HowExpert Guide to Artificial Intelligence

101+ Lessons to Explore Technologies, Impact, and the Evolutionary Journey in the AI Revolution

HowExpert

For more tips related to this topic, visit HowExpert.com/ai.

Recommended Resources

- HowExpert.com – How To Guides on All Topics from A to Z by Everyday Experts.
- HowExpert.com/free – Free HowExpert Email Newsletter.
- HowExpert.com/books – HowExpert Books
- HowExpert.com/courses – HowExpert Courses
- HowExpert.com/clothing – HowExpert Clothing
- HowExpert.com/membership – HowExpert Membership Site
- HowExpert.com/affiliates – HowExpert Affiliate Program
- HowExpert.com/jobs – HowExpert Jobs
- HowExpert.com/writers – Write About Your #1 Passion/Knowledge/Expertise & Become a HowExpert Author.
- HowExpert.com/resources – Additional HowExpert Recommended Resources
- YouTube.com/HowExpert – Subscribe to HowExpert YouTube.
- Instagram.com/HowExpert – Follow HowExpert on Instagram.
- Facebook.com/HowExpert – Follow HowExpert on Facebook.
- TikTok.com/@HowExpert – Follow HowExpert on TikTok.

Publisher's Foreword

Dear HowExpert Reader,

HowExpert publishes quick 'how to' guides on all topics from A to Z by everyday experts.

At HowExpert, our mission is to discover, empower, and maximize everyday people's talents to ultimately make a positive impact in the world for all topics from A to Z...one everyday expert at a time!

HowExpert guides are written by everyday people just like you and me, who have a passion, knowledge, and expertise for a specific topic.

We take great pride in selecting everyday experts who have a passion, real-life experience in a topic, and excellent writing skills to teach you about the topic you are also passionate about and eager to learn.

We hope you get a lot of value from our HowExpert guides, and it can make a positive impact on your life in some way. All of our readers, including you, help us continue living our mission of positively impacting the world for all spheres of influences from A to Z.

If you enjoyed one of our HowExpert guides, then please take a moment to send us your feedback from wherever you got this book.

Thank you, and we wish you all the best in all aspects of life.

To your success,

Byungjoon "BJ" Min / 민병준
Founder & Publisher of HowExpert
HowExpert.com

PS...If you are also interested in becoming a HowExpert author, then please visit our website at HowExpert.com/writers. Thank you & again, all the best! John 3:16

Table of Contents

Recommended Resources 2

Publisher's Foreword...3

Preface: Navigating the Transformative Journey of AI 13

   1. Introduction to the Preface 13

   2. Insights into the Transformative Journey of AI.......................13

   3. The Purpose of This Exploration.......................................13

   4. The Promise of This Exploration.......................................13

   5. Conclusion of the Preface 14

Introduction: Unraveling the Allure of Artificial Intelligence..........15

   1. The Allure of Artificial Intelligence: Myths and Realities 15

   2. Overview of the Book's Structure 15

   3. Key Objectives of the Book 16

   4. Conclusion 16

Part I: The Essence of AI 17

Chapter 1: The Genesis of AI 17

   1.1   The Concept and Inception of Artificial Intelligence 17

      1.1.1   The Conception of AI: The Turing Test (1950)............17

      1.1.2   The Birth of AI: Dartmouth Conference (1956) 18

      1.1.3   Early AI Programs: ELIZA and SHRDLU 18

      1.1.4   The Rise of Machine Learning: Decision Trees (1980s) 18

      1.1.5   The Emergence of Neural Networks: Backpropagation (1986) 18

      1.1.6   Deep Learning Revolution: AlexNet (2012) 19

      1.1.7   AI Mastery in Games: DeepMind's AlphaGo (2016)...19

      1.1.8   AI for Language Understanding: GPT-3 (2020) 19

      1.1.9   Conclusion..19

   1.2   Milestones in the AI odyssey. 20

      1.2.1   Alan Turing and the Turing Test (1950):....................20

      1.2.2   The Dartmouth Conference (1956):...........................20

      1.2.3   The Perceptron and Neural Networks (1957):.............21

      1.2.4   Expert Systems and Knowledge Representation (1970s-1980s): 21

1.2.5   Deep Blue vs. Garry Kasparov (1997): 21

1.2.6   The Deep Learning Revolution (2012): 22

1.2.7   AlphaGo and Reinforcement Learning (2016): 22

1.2.8   Future Horizons: 22

1.2.9   Conclusion: 23

1.3   Pioneers and Visionaries of AI 23

1.3.1   Alan Turing (1912-1954): 24

1.3.2   John McCarthy (1927-2011): 24

1.3.3   Marvin Minsky (1927-2016): 24

1.3.4   Herbert Simon (1916-2001): 25

1.3.5   Grace Hopper (1906-1992): 25

1.3.6   Yoshua Bengio (1964-present): 25

1.3.7   Fei-Fei Li (1976-present): 26

1.3.8   Arthur Samuel (1901-1990): 26

1.3.9   Yann LeCun (1960-present): 26

1.3.10   Andrew Ng (1976-present): 27

1.3.11   Conclusion: 27

Chapter Review 27

Chapter 2: AI Decoded 33

2.1   Defining Artificial Intelligence 33

2.1.1   Essential Characteristics of AI 33

2.2   Core Components of AI Systems 34

2.2.1   Fundamental Elements of AI 35

2.3   The Spectrum of AI: From Narrow to General Intelligence   36

2.3.1   Diverse Categories of AI.. 36

Chapter Review 38

Part II: Technologies Driving AI 41

Chapter 3: Machine Learning – The Backbone of AI 41

3.1 Introduction to Machine Learning 41

3.1.1   Core Principles and Mechanisms 41

3.1.2   Types of Machine Learning.................................... 42

3.1.3   Operational Mechanisms 43

3.2 Key Machine Learning Algorithms............................. 44

3.2.1   Supervised Learning Algorithms 44

3.2.2   Unsupervised Learning Algorithms........................45

3.2.3   Reinforcement Learning Algorithms.......................45

3.2.4   Specialized Algorithms 46

3.3   Real-world Applications of Machine Learning 47

3.3.1   Transformative Sectors.....................................47

3.3.2   Impactful Applications... 49

Chapter Review... 50

Chapter 4: Deep Learning – AI's Deep Mind...............................53

4.1   Unraveling Deep Learning..53

4.1.1   Conceptual Foundations 53

4.1.2   Mechanisms of Learning......................................54

4.2   Architecture of Neural Networks.................................55

4.2.1   Structural Overview 55

4.2.2   Diverse Architectures...56

4.2.3   Advanced Techniques 57

4.3   Breakthroughs Enabled by Deep Learning 58

4.3.1   Revolution in Perception 58

4.3.2   Mastery of Language...59

4.3.3   Autonomous Navigation 59

4.3.4   Healthcare Innovations 59

4.3.5   Game-Changing Strategies 60

Chapter Review... 61

Chapter 5: Other AI Technologies... 64

5.1   Natural Language Processing (NLP) 64

5.1.1   Key Areas of NLP 64

5.1.2   Impact and Applications 65

5.1.3   Conclusion.. 66

5.2 Robotics and Autonomous Systems 67

5.2.1   Key Components 67

5.2.2   Impact and Applications 68

5.2.3   Conclusion.. 69

5.3 Augmented and Virtual Reality in AI 69

5.3.1   Key Aspects 69

5.3.2   Impact and Applications 70

5.3.3   Conclusion 71

Chapter Review 72

Part III: AI in Action 75

Chapter 6: AI in Everyday Life 75

6.1   Personal Assistants and Smart Homes 75

6.1.1   Personal Assistants: Revolutionizing Interaction and Convenience 75

6.1.2   Smart Homes: Automating and Enhancing Living Spaces 76

6.1.3   Future Directions: Envisioning Next-Generation Smart Living 76

6.1.4   Conclusion 77

6.2   AI in Entertainment and Gaming 77

6.2.1   Personalized Content Discovery 77

6.2.2   Enhanced Viewer Engagement 78

6.2.3   Revolutionizing Gaming 78

6.2.4   Future Trends in AI-Driven Entertainment 79

6.2.5   Conclusion 79

6.3   The Future of Mobility: Autonomous Vehicles 80

6.3.1   Technological Foundations of Autonomous Vehicles 80

6.3.2   Impact on Society and Urban Environments 80

6.3.3   Challenges and Considerations for the Future 81

6.3.4   Looking Ahead: The Road to Autonomous Futures 81

6.3.5   Conclusion 82

Chapter Review 82

Chapter 7: AI in Industry 85

7.1 Transforming Healthcare with AI 85

7.1.1   Diagnostic Innovations 85

7.2 AI in Finance: From Fraud Detection to Robo-Advisors 87

7.2.1   Enhancing Security with Fraud Detection 88

7.2.2. Personalized Financial Services 88

7.3 The Role of AI in Manufacturing and Supply Chains 90

7.3.1. Optimizing Production Processes 90

7.3.2. Supply Chain Optimization 91

Chapter Review 93

Chapter 8: Ethical and Societal Impacts of AI 95

8.1 Navigating the Ethical Landscape of AI 95

8.1.1   Fairness and Bias 96

8.1.2   Accountability and Transparency 96

8.1.3   Ethical Decision-Making..97

8.2 AI and the Future of Work 98

8.2.1   Job Displacement and Creation................................... 98

8.2.2   Skill Shifts and Education... 99

8.2.3   Worker Empowerment vs. Surveillance 99

8.3 Ensuring Privacy and Security in an AI-driven World 100

8.3.1   Data Privacy 101

8.3.2   Security Against AI Threats 101

8.3.3   Ethical Use of Surveillance Technologies.................. 102

Chapter Review 103

Part IV: Creating and Managing AI 106

Chapter 9: Developing AI Solutions... 106

9.1   Building Blocks of AI Development 106

9.1.1   Data 106

9.1.2   Algorithms.. 106

9.1.3   Computing Power.. 107

9.1.4   Expertise.. 107

9.2   Tools and Frameworks for AI Creation 107

9.2.1   Machine Learning Libraries..................................... 108

9.2.2   Integrated Development Environments (IDEs)........ 108

9.2.3   Cloud AI Services 109

9.3   Best Practices in AI Project Management 110

9.3.1   Clearly Define Objectives and Scope: 110

9.3.2   Embrace Agile Methodologies: 110

9.3.3   Focus on Data Quality:.. 110

9.3.4   Ethical and Responsible AI:..................................... 111

9.3.5   Continuous Testing and Evaluation: 111

Chapter Review 111

Chapter 10: AI and Global Challenges 114

10.1 AI's Role in Addressing Climate Change 114

    10.1.1   Understanding the Significance of Climate Change:.. 114

    10.1.2   Harnessing AI Technologies for Climate Solutions: . 114

    10.1.3   Optimizing Resource Allocation and Sustainability: 115

    10.1.4   Facilitating Climate Adaptation and Resilience:....... 115

10.2 Leveraging AI for Global Health...................................... 116

    10.2.1   Advancements in Medical Diagnosis and Treatment: 116

    10.2.2   Enhancing Access to Healthcare Services:............. 116

    10.2.3   Disease Surveillance and Prevention: 116

    10.2.4   Ethical and Regulatory Considerations: 117

10.3 AI in the Service of Education and Equity 117

    10.3.1   Personalized Learning Experiences:......................... 118

    10.3.2   Optimized Curriculum Design: 118

    10.3.3   Expanding Access to Quality Education: 118

    10.3.4   Addressing Equity and Inclusion: 119

Chapter Review 119

Part V: The Horizon of AI... 121

Chapter 11: The Frontier of AI Research................................. 121

11.1   Cutting-edge Research in AI... 121

    11.1.1   Continuous Innovation: 121

    11.1.2   Areas of Focus: 121

    11.1.3   Remarkable Achievements: 122

11.2   AI's Quest for Understanding Human Intelligence 123

    11.2.1   Ultimate Goal:...123

    11.2.2   Interdisciplinary Approach:......................................123

    11.2.3   Challenges and Considerations: 123

11.3. Challenges and Opportunities in AI Advancement...........124

    11.3.1   Challenges in AI Advancement:..............................124

    11.3.2   Opportunities in AI Advancement:.........................125

    11.3.3   Importance of Addressing Challenges and Seizing
Opportunities: 125

Chapter Review 126

Chapter 12: The Future Shaped by AI 128

12.1   Visioning the AI-augmented Future..............................128

12.1.1   AI Integration:...128

12.1.2   Automation and Job Evolution: 128

12.1.3   Personalized Experiences: 128

12.2   AI's Potential Societal Transformations 129

12.2.1   Impact on Healthcare: 129

12.2.2   Economic Disruption: 129

12.2.3   Environmental Sustainability: 130

12.3   Ethical AI: Guiding Principles for a New Era 130

12.3.1   Transparency and Accountability:...........................130

12.3.2   Fairness and Equity:...131

12.3.3   Human-Centered Design:.....................................131

Chapter Review 131

Frequently Asked Questions 134

Introduction to AI...134

What is Artificial Intelligence (AI)?..................................134

How are AI, Machine Learning (ML), and Deep Learning (DL) related?..134

Applications of AI Across Industries....................................134

Healthcare: How is AI transforming healthcare? 134

Finance: What impact does AI have on the finance industry? 134

Education: Can AI improve educational outcomes? 135

Agriculture: How does AI benefit agriculture? 135

Manufacturing: What role does AI play in manufacturing? ..135

AI in Business and Economics 135

Marketing: How does AI influence marketing strategies?.....135

Supply Chain Management: What advantages does AI offer in supply chain management? 135

Societal Implications of AI 136

Ethical Concerns: What ethical issues are associated with AI? 136

Bias Mitigation: How can AI bias be addressed? 136

The Future of AI & Education 136

    Emerging Trends: What are the latest trends in AI? 136

    Education and Careers: How is AI shaping the future of
    education and careers? 136

    Future Evolution: How will AI evolve in the coming years?..137

Conclusion 138

  Reflecting on AI's Evolution 138

  The Technical Backbone and Its Capacities 138

  AI's Multifaceted Applications 138

  Navigating Ethical and Societal Terrains 139

  Looking Ahead: The Future Shaped by AI 139

  A Journey That Continues 139

  Epilogue: The Continuous Learning Path 139

Epilogue 141

Appendices 142

  I.   Glossary of AI Terms A to Z 142

  II.   AI Resource Guide 146

  III.   Interviews with AI Experts 147

Acknowledgments 149

About the Book 152

About the Publisher..154

Recommended Resources 155

Preface: Navigating the Transformative Journey of AI

1. Introduction to the Preface

- The preface sets the stage for a deep dive into the transformative world of artificial intelligence (AI), promising to guide readers through the fascinating evolution of this field. It aims to not only educate but also inspire by showcasing the vast potential AI holds for shaping our future.

2. Insights into the Transformative Journey of AI

- The journey of AI from its conceptual inception to its current state as a cornerstone of technological advancement is nothing short of remarkable. This section provides a compelling overview of how AI has evolved, highlighting key milestones and breakthroughs that have significantly impacted various sectors, including healthcare, finance, education, and more. Through these insights, readers gain an appreciation for the depth and breadth of AI's influence on our world.

3. The Purpose of This Exploration

- The primary goal of this exploration is to demystify AI for a broad audience, from students and enthusiasts to professionals and scholars. By breaking down complex concepts into accessible insights, the book aims to illuminate the inner workings of AI technologies and their applications. This exploration seeks to empower readers with a thorough understanding of AI, enabling them to appreciate its capabilities, challenges, and future possibilities.

4. The Promise of This Exploration

- Beyond merely providing information, this exploration promises to engage readers in a thought-provoking journey that examines the ethical, societal, and technological implications of AI. It aims to foster a critical understanding of AI's role in our lives, encouraging readers to reflect on how they can contribute to or shape the development of AI technologies. The promise extends to offering a vision of the future, where AI's potential to transform our world is fully realized, guiding principles for ethical AI development, and a call to action for responsible innovation.

5. *Conclusion of the Preface*

- Concluding the preface, there is a reaffirmation of the exploration's objectives: to educate, inspire, and provoke thoughtful consideration of AI's impact on society. Readers are invited to embark on this journey with an open mind, ready to explore the multifaceted dimensions of AI. The preface assures that, by the end of this exploration, readers will have a comprehensive understanding of AI, equipped with the knowledge to navigate its evolving landscape confidently.

By systematically presenting the transformative journey of AI, the purpose and promise of this exploration, this preface lays the groundwork for a profound and enlightening journey into the world of artificial intelligence. It sets a high expectation for the content that follows, promising a blend of educational depth, inspirational stories, and thoughtful reflections on the future of AI.

Introduction: Unraveling the Allure of Artificial Intelligence

1. The Allure of Artificial Intelligence: Myths and Realities

- The introduction begins by addressing the dual nature of artificial intelligence (AI)—its allure. This allure is twofold: on one hand, there are the myths, the sensationalized portrayals of AI that dominate popular culture, suggesting a future where AI surpasses human intelligence and potentially poses existential threats. On the other hand, there are the realities, grounded in current research and applications, showing AI as a powerful tool that, while transformative, is still under human direction and far from the omnipotent force often depicted. This section demystifies AI, separating fact from fiction and setting the stage for a grounded exploration of AI's capabilities and limitations.

2. Overview of the Book's Structure

- Following the discussion of AI's myths and realities, the introduction provides a detailed overview of the book's structure, which is meticulously designed to guide readers through the multifaceted world of AI. The structure is presented as follows:
- Part I: The Essence of AI covers the historical evolution, fundamental concepts, and the visionaries behind AI's development.
- Part II: Technologies Driving AI dives into the core technologies that power AI, such as machine learning and deep learning, and their applications.
- Part III: AI in Action showcases practical applications of AI in various sectors and its impact on daily life.
- Part IV: Creating and Managing AI focuses on the development, management, and ethical considerations of AI technologies.
- Part V: The Horizon of AI looks to the future, exploring emerging research areas, potential societal transformations, and ethical frameworks for AI.

3. Key Objectives of the Book

- The introduction then outlines the key objectives of the book, which include:
- Educating readers about AI's principles, history, and technological underpinnings.
- Debunking common myths and clarifying the current state and capabilities of AI.
- Highlighting AI's practical applications and the positive impacts it can have on society.
- Addressing ethical considerations and promoting a dialogue on the future direction of AI development.
- Inspiring readers to engage with AI, whether through further study, career paths, or informed discussions on its societal implications.

4. Conclusion

- The book concludes by emphasizing the importance of understanding AI in today's technology-driven world. It invites readers to embark on this comprehensive journey with an open mind, prepared to explore the realities of AI beyond the myths. By setting clear expectations for the book's content and objectives, the introduction ensures that readers are well-prepared for a deep and balanced exploration of artificial intelligence.

By systematically addressing the allure of AI, providing a detailed overview of the book's structure, and outlining its key objectives, the introduction to "Navigating the AI Horizon: Myths, Realities, and the Future" prepares readers for an engaging and enlightening journey into the world of artificial intelligence. It sets the stage for a nuanced understanding of AI, promising a blend of educational insights, practical applications, and thoughtful discussions on the ethical and societal implications of AI technologies.

Part I: The Essence of AI

Chapter 1: The Genesis of AI

In the vast and ever-expanding universe of technology, the concept of artificial intelligence (AI) has stood out as a beacon of innovation and futuristic possibility. At the intersection of computer science, cognitive psychology, and engineering, AI has grown from a mere idea into a pivotal force that is reshaping every aspect of human life. This chapter embarks on a journey through the origins, evolution, and key figures of AI, tracing its transformation from theoretical musings to a dynamic field that continues to challenge the boundaries of what machines can achieve.

1.1 The Concept and Inception of Artificial Intelligence

The journey of Artificial Intelligence (AI) is marked by groundbreaking milestones that have not only defined the course of technological advancement but also reshaped societal perceptions and applications of intelligent machines. This odyssey from theoretical foundations to transformative technologies highlights the rapid pace of innovation and the profound impact of AI on the modern world.

1.1.1 The Conception of AI: The Turing Test (1950)

Proposed by Alan Turing in his seminal paper "Computing Machinery and Intelligence," the Turing Test established a criterion for determining whether a machine could exhibit intelligent behavior equivalent to, or indistinguishable from, that of a human.

1.1.2   *The Birth of AI: Dartmouth Conference (1956)*

A proposal by John McCarthy, Marvin Minsky, Nathaniel Rochester, and Claude Shannon led to the Dartmouth Conference, where "Artificial Intelligence" was coined as a term and recognized as a distinct field of research. This event is widely considered the official birth of AI as a discipline.

1.1.3   *Early AI Programs: ELIZA and SHRDLU*

- *ELIZA (1966)*

Developed by Joseph Weizenbaum, ELIZA was one of the first chatbots and a early demonstration of the potential for machines to mimic human conversation, despite lacking true understanding.

- *SHRDLU (1970)*

Created by Terry Winograd, SHRDLU was a natural language understanding computer program that could interact with a user in English about a world of blocks of various shapes and sizes, showcasing the ability of machines to parse and respond to human language in restricted domains.

1.1.4   *The Rise of Machine Learning: Decision Trees (1980s)*

The 1980s saw the introduction of decision trees for machine learning, enabling computers to learn from data and make decisions based on statistical patterns. This marked a shift towards data-driven AI.

1.1.5   *The Emergence of Neural Networks: Backpropagation (1986)*

The development of the backpropagation algorithm by David Rumelhart, Geoffrey Hinton, and Ronald Williams allowed neural networks to adjust their parameters to improve performance. This breakthrough laid the foundation for deep learning.

1.1.6 *Deep Learning Revolution: AlexNet (2012)*

A deep neural network designed by Alex Krizhevsky, Ilya Sutskever, and Geoffrey Hinton, AlexNet won the 2012 ImageNet Large Scale Visual Recognition Challenge by a large margin. This success demonstrated the power of deep learning, revitalizing interest in neural networks and significantly advancing the field of computer vision.

1.1.7 *AI Mastery in Games: DeepMind's AlphaGo (2016)*

Developed by Google's DeepMind, AlphaGo defeated world champion Go player Lee Sedol in 2016. This was a landmark event, as Go is a complex board game requiring intuition and strategy, showcasing AI's ability to master tasks once considered beyond its reach.

1.1.8 *AI for Language Understanding: GPT-3 (2020)*

OpenAI's GPT-3, with its 175 billion parameters, became the most advanced natural language processing model upon its release. Demonstrating a remarkable ability to generate human-like text, GPT-3 pushed the boundaries of AI's capabilities in understanding and generating human language.

1.1.9 *Conclusion*

The AI odyssey is a testament to human ingenuity and the relentless pursuit of knowledge. From the foundational Turing Test to the latest advances in deep learning and natural language processing, each milestone represents a leap forward in our ability to endow machines with intelligence. As we continue to explore the potential of AI, these milestones serve as both markers of our progress and beacons guiding us toward a future where AI and human intelligence collaborate in shaping a new era of innovation and discovery.

1.2 Milestones in the AI odyssey.

Artificial Intelligence (AI) stands as a testament to human innovation, with its evolution marked by pivotal milestones achieved through the dedication and ingenuity of visionary leaders. These milestones not only signify advancements in technology but also embody the collective effort to unlock the potential of intelligent machines. Let us embark on a journey through the significant milestones in the AI odyssey, paying homage to the remarkable figures whose contributions have shaped the AI landscape.

1.2.1 Alan Turing and the Turing Test (1950):

- Alan Turing, a British mathematician and computer scientist, proposed the Turing Test in his seminal paper, "Computing Machinery and Intelligence."
- The Turing Test served as a benchmark for evaluating a machine's ability to exhibit human-like intelligence, igniting discussions on the nature of AI and machine cognition.
- Turing's pioneering work laid the groundwork for AI research and inspired generations of scientists to explore the possibilities of machine intelligence.

1.2.2 The Dartmouth Conference (1956):

- The Dartmouth Conference, convened by John McCarthy, Marvin Minsky, Allen Newell, and Herbert Simon, marked the formal establishment of AI as an interdisciplinary field of study.
- Participants at the conference outlined the objectives and scope of AI research, laying the foundation for future advancements in artificial intelligence.

- The Dartmouth Conference catalyzed collaboration among scientists from various disciplines, fostering an environment conducive to innovation and discovery.

1.2.3 *The Perceptron and Neural Networks (1957):*

- Frank Rosenblatt's development of the Perceptron introduced the concept of artificial neural networks, drawing inspiration from the structure and function of the human brain.
- The Perceptron demonstrated the potential of machine learning and pattern recognition, sparking interest in neural network research.
- Although the initial enthusiasm surrounding the Perceptron waned, it paved the way for the resurgence of neural network research in subsequent decades.

1.2.4 *Expert Systems and Knowledge Representation (1970s-1980s):*

- Edward Feigenbaum, Joshua Lederberg, and their colleagues pioneered the development of expert systems, AI programs designed to emulate human expertise in specific domains.
- Expert systems utilized knowledge representation techniques to encode domain-specific knowledge and reasoning methods to solve complex problems.
- The advent of expert systems showcased the practical applications of AI in fields such as medicine, finance, and engineering, revolutionizing decision-making processes.

1.2.5 *Deep Blue vs. Garry Kasparov (1997):*

- IBM's Deep Blue made history by defeating world chess champion Garry Kasparov in a highly publicized match.
- Deep Blue's victory underscored the potential of AI to excel in strategic decision-making and computational intelligence.
- The match captured global attention and stimulated interest in AI research, driving advancements in machine learning algorithms and game-playing systems.

1.2.6   *The Deep Learning Revolution (2012):*

- The ImageNet Large Scale Visual Recognition Challenge in 2012 marked a significant breakthrough in AI research, with Alex Krizhevsky, Ilya Sutskever, and Geoffrey Hinton's convolutional neural network, AlexNet, achieving remarkable success in image classification tasks.
- The success of deep learning techniques revolutionized computer vision, natural language processing, and other AI domains, leading to unprecedented advancements in AI capabilities.
- The deep learning revolution propelled AI into new frontiers, enabling machines to perceive and understand the world with unprecedented accuracy and efficiency.

1.2.7   *AlphaGo and Reinforcement Learning (2016):*

- DeepMind's AlphaGo made headlines by defeating world Go champion Lee Sedol in a historic match, showcasing the capabilities of AI in mastering complex strategic games.
- AlphaGo's success was attributed to its use of reinforcement learning techniques, which enabled it to learn from experience and improve its gameplay over time.
- The victory of AlphaGo marked a significant milestone in AI research, demonstrating the potential of reinforcement learning in training intelligent agents and solving complex decision-making problems.

1.2.8   *Future Horizons:*

- Looking ahead, the future of AI holds immense promise and potential, with advancements poised to revolutionize various aspects of society and technology.
- Ethical considerations will play a pivotal role in guiding the responsible development and deployment of AI systems, ensuring alignment with human values and societal well-being.
- Human-AI collaboration will redefine industries and professions, augmenting human capabilities and fostering innovation across diverse sectors.

- Quantum computing stands as a transformative frontier in AI, offering unprecedented processing power and enabling breakthroughs in complex problem-solving and optimization.
- AI-driven personalized medicine will revolutionize healthcare, with tailored treatments and predictive analytics improving patient outcomes and healthcare delivery.
- Autonomous systems powered by AI will reshape transportation, manufacturing, and logistics, driving efficiency and innovation in global supply chains.
- AI-driven sustainability solutions will address pressing environmental challenges, leveraging data-driven insights to mitigate climate change and promote ecological resilience.
- Continued research in AI safety and robustness will mitigate risks associated with AI deployment, ensuring the reliability, security, and transparency of AI systems.
- As we embark on this future trajectory, it is essential to remain mindful of the ethical, social, and economic implications of AI, striving for inclusive and equitable progress that benefits all of humanity.

1.2.9   *Conclusion:*

The AI odyssey is a testament to human ingenuity and perseverance, with each milestone representing a leap forward in our quest to unlock the mysteries of intelligence. From Alan Turing's conceptualization of machine cognition to DeepMind's triumph with AlphaGo, visionary leaders have continuously pushed the boundaries of what machines can achieve. As we honor these pioneers and visionaries, we also look ahead with anticipation, eager to witness the next chapter in the AI odyssey and the transformative impact it will bring to our world.

1.3   *Pioneers and Visionaries of AI*

The evolution of Artificial Intelligence (AI) has been shaped by the relentless pursuit of knowledge and innovation by visionary individuals. From the foundational work of early pioneers to the groundbreaking research of contemporary leaders, these trailblazers have transformed AI from a theoretical concept into a powerful force driving technological progress. Let's explore the lives and legacies of some of the most influential figures in the field of AI.

1.3.1   *Alan Turing (1912-1954):*

- Alan Turing, a British mathematician, is hailed as the father of computer science and AI for his pioneering work in computation and machine intelligence.
- His conceptualization of the Turing Test laid the groundwork for evaluating machine intelligence and sparked the development of AI as a field of study.
- Turing's contributions during World War II, particularly his efforts in code-breaking with the Enigma machine, demonstrated the potential of machine-based computation.

1.3.2   *John McCarthy (1927-2011):*

- John McCarthy, an American computer scientist, coined the term "Artificial Intelligence" and organized the seminal Dartmouth Conference in 1956, marking the birth of AI as a field.
- His visionary leadership and advocacy for AI as an interdisciplinary endeavor laid the foundation for decades of research and development in the field.
- McCarthy's contributions to symbolic AI and knowledge representation paved the way for the development of expert systems and early AI programs.

1.3.3   *Marvin Minsky (1927-2016):*

- Marvin Minsky, an American cognitive scientist, was a pioneer in the study of artificial neural networks and cognitive architectures.
- His work on the perceptron and the development of early neural network models laid the groundwork for modern machine learning and deep learning techniques.
- Minsky's interdisciplinary approach to AI research, integrating insights from neuroscience and psychology, enriched the field and inspired generations of researchers.

1.3.4   _Herbert Simon (1916-2001):_

- Herbert Simon, an American economist and cognitive psychologist, made significant contributions to AI through his research on decision-making processes.
- His work on early AI programs, such as the Logic Theorist and the General Problem Solver, demonstrated AI's ability to solve complex problems and simulate human reasoning.
- Simon's interdisciplinary perspective, combining AI with economics and psychology, advanced our understanding of human cognition and laid the groundwork for AI applications in various domains.

1.3.5   _Grace Hopper (1906-1992):_

- Grace Hopper, an American computer scientist and U.S. Navy rear admiral, was a pioneer in computer programming languages and compiler development.
- Her work on the development of the UNIVAC I compiler paved the way for high-level programming languages and revolutionized the field of computing.
- Hopper's advocacy for machine-independent programming languages, exemplified by her work on COBOL, democratized access to computing and catalyzed advancements in AI research.

1.3.6   _Yoshua Bengio (1964-present):_

- Yoshua Bengio, a Canadian computer scientist, is a leading figure in the field of deep learning and neural networks.
- His research on deep learning algorithms and neural network architectures has significantly contributed to advancements in AI, particularly in areas such as natural language processing and reinforcement learning.
- Bengio's work has laid the foundation for practical applications of deep learning in various domains, including healthcare, finance, and autonomous driving.

1.3.7 *Fei-Fei Li (1976-present):*

- Fei-Fei Li, a Chinese-American computer scientist, is renowned for her contributions to computer vision and machine learning.
- Her research on visual recognition and image understanding has advanced the field of computer vision, enabling breakthroughs in object recognition, scene understanding, and visual reasoning.
- Li's efforts have led to the development of large-scale datasets and benchmarking tools, facilitating progress in computer vision research and applications.

1.3.8 *Arthur Samuel (1901-1990):*

- Arthur Samuel, an American computer scientist, is considered a pioneer in the field of machine learning and artificial intelligence.
- His development of the Samuel Checkers-playing Program, which learned to play checkers through self-play and reinforcement learning, marked an early milestone in AI research.
- Samuel's work laid the foundation for the field of machine learning and inspired subsequent generations of researchers to explore the potential of computational learning algorithms.

1.3.9 *Yann LeCun (1960-present):*

- Yann LeCun, a French-American computer scientist, is known for his contributions to convolutional neural networks (CNNs) and deep learning.
- His research on CNNs has revolutionized computer vision and pattern recognition, leading to breakthroughs in image classification, object detection, and facial recognition.
- LeCun's work has had a profound impact on various AI applications, including autonomous driving, medical imaging, and robotics.

1.3.10   *Andrew Ng (1976-present):*

- Andrew Ng, a British-American computer scientist, is a leading figure in the field of AI and machine learning.
- His work on online education platforms, such as Coursera, has democratized access to AI education and training, empowering individuals worldwide to learn and apply AI skills.
- Ng's research on deep learning algorithms and online learning methods has advanced the state-of-the-art in AI and contributed to the development of practical AI applications.

1.3.11   *Conclusion:*

The contributions of these pioneers and visionaries have shaped the trajectory of AI, from its inception to the present day. Their groundbreaking research, innovative ideas, and tireless dedication have laid the foundation for the advancements that continue to propel the field forward. As we honor their legacies, we recognize the profound impact they have had on shaping the future of technology and society through AI.

Chapter Review

1.1 The Concept and Inception of Artificial Intelligence

Artificial Intelligence (AI) is the endeavor to create machines capable of intelligent behavior. The genesis of AI as a scientific discipline can be traced back to the mid-20th century, though the fascination with creating artificial beings with intelligence has ancient roots. The formal inception occurred during a Dartmouth College conference in 1956, where the term "Artificial Intelligence" was coined by John McCarthy. This event marked the official birth of AI as a field of study, setting the stage for decades of research, development, and philosophical debate about the nature of intelligence and the possibility of replicating such a phenomenon mechanically or digitally.

1.2 Milestones in the AI Odyssey

This section delves into the transformative journey of Artificial Intelligence (AI), highlighting key milestones and the visionary individuals behind them. It emphasizes the pivotal role played by pioneers and visionaries in shaping the landscape of AI, from its conceptualization to its current state of advancement.

1. Alan Turing and the Turing Test (1950):

- The chapter commences with an exploration of Alan Turing's groundbreaking work on the Turing Test, which laid the foundation for AI research.
- Turing's seminal paper, "Computing Machinery and Intelligence," sparked discussions on machine intelligence and set the stage for subsequent developments in AI.

2. The Dartmouth Conference (1956):

- The narrative then shifts to the Dartmouth Conference, a historic event that formalized AI as a distinct field of study.
- Attendees, including John McCarthy, Marvin Minsky, Allen Newell, and Herbert Simon, outlined the objectives and scope of AI research, fostering collaboration and innovation.

3. The Perceptron and Neural Networks (1957):

- The chapter explores Frank Rosenblatt's creation of the Perceptron, which introduced the concept of artificial neural networks.
- Rosenblatt's pioneering work laid the groundwork for advancements in machine learning and pattern recognition, sparking renewed interest in neural network research.

4. Expert Systems and Knowledge Representation (1970s-1980s):

- Next, the narrative examines the development of expert systems, AI programs designed to emulate human expertise in specific domains.
- Edward Feigenbaum, Joshua Lederberg, and others showcased the practical applications of AI in fields such as medicine and finance, revolutionizing decision-making processes.

5. Deep Blue vs. Garry Kasparov (1997):

- The chapter discusses IBM's Deep Blue's historic victory over world chess champion Garry Kasparov, highlighting AI's prowess in strategic decision-making.
- Deep Blue's success captured global attention and stimulated interest in AI research, driving advancements in machine learning algorithms and game-playing systems.

6. The Deep Learning Revolution (2012):

- The narrative explores the deep learning revolution ignited by the ImageNet Challenge in 2012, where AlexNet achieved unprecedented success in image classification tasks.
- Alex Krizhevsky, Ilya Sutskever, and Geoffrey Hinton's breakthrough paved the way for advancements in computer vision, natural language processing, and other AI domains.

7. AlphaGo and Reinforcement Learning (2016):

- Finally, the chapter highlights DeepMind's AlphaGo's victory over world Go champion Lee Sedol, showcasing the capabilities of AI in mastering complex strategic games.
- AlphaGo's success with reinforcement learning techniques marked a significant milestone in AI research, demonstrating the potential of intelligent agents in solving complex decision-making problems.

8. Future Horizons:

- The future of AI holds tremendous promise for revolutionizing society and technology.
- Ethical considerations will guide responsible development, ensuring alignment with human values. Human-AI collaboration will drive innovation across industries, while quantum computing unlocks unprecedented processing power.
- AI-driven personalized medicine will transform healthcare, improving patient outcomes and delivery.
- Autonomous systems will innovate transportation and supply chains. AI will address environmental challenges and enhance sustainability efforts.

- Continued research in AI safety will ensure reliability and security.
- It's imperative to consider the ethical, social, and economic impacts of AI, striving for inclusive progress that benefits humanity.

This section concludes by emphasizing the collective impact of these milestones on the evolution of AI and the profound influence of visionary leaders in driving progress. It underscores the importance of honoring the contributions of pioneers and visionaries while looking ahead to the future of AI, filled with promise and possibility.

1.3 Pioneers and Visionaries of AI

This section sets the tone by highlighting the transformative impact of visionary individuals in shaping the evolution of Artificial Intelligence (AI). It emphasizes the relentless pursuit of knowledge and innovation displayed by these trailblazers, from the early pioneers to contemporary leaders. The introduction establishes the purpose of the exploration - to delve into the lives and legacies of some of the most influential figures in the field of AI.

1. Alan Turing (1912-1954):

- Alan Turing, renowned as the father of computer science and AI, laid the groundwork for evaluating machine intelligence through the Turing Test.
- His contributions to code-breaking during World War II showcased the potential of machine-based computation, shaping modern computing and AI.

2. John McCarthy (1927-2011):

- John McCarthy's visionary leadership and advocacy for AI as an interdisciplinary field marked the birth of AI at the seminal Dartmouth Conference.
- His contributions to symbolic AI and knowledge representation laid the foundation for decades of research and development in AI.

3. Marvin Minsky (1927-2016):

- Marvin Minsky's pioneering work in artificial neural networks and cognitive architectures revolutionized AI research.
- His interdisciplinary approach enriched the field, inspiring generations of researchers and laying the groundwork for modern machine learning techniques.

4. Herbert Simon (1916-2001):

- Herbert Simon's research on decision-making processes demonstrated AI's problem-solving capabilities and integrated AI with economics and psychology.
- His interdisciplinary perspective advanced our understanding of human cognition and laid the groundwork for AI applications in various domains.

5. Grace Hopper (1906-1992):

- Grace Hopper's contributions to computer programming languages and compiler development democratized access to computing and catalyzed advancements in AI research.
- Her advocacy for machine-independent programming languages revolutionized the field of computing.

6. Yoshua Bengio (1964-present):

- Yoshua Bengio's groundbreaking work in deep learning and neural networks has significantly advanced AI research.
- His contributions have laid the foundation for practical applications of deep learning across various domains, shaping the future of AI.

7. Fei-Fei Li (1976-present):

- Fei-Fei Li's expertise in computer vision and machine learning has led to breakthrough advancements in AI.
- Her research has facilitated progress in computer vision research and applications, shaping the field's capabilities in image understanding.

8. Arthur Samuel (1901-1990):

-   Arthur Samuel's development of the Samuel Checkers-playing Program marked a significant milestone in AI research.
-   His work laid the foundation for the field of machine learning, inspiring subsequent generations of researchers to explore computational learning algorithms.

9. Yann LeCun (1960-present):

-   Yann LeCun's research in convolutional neural networks and deep learning has revolutionized computer vision and pattern recognition.
-   His contributions have had a profound impact on various AI applications, driving advancements in fields such as autonomous driving and medical imaging.

10. Andrew Ng (1976-present):

-   Andrew Ng's leadership in AI education and research has democratized access to AI knowledge and skills.
-   His work has empowered individuals worldwide to learn and apply AI concepts, contributing to the advancement of AI research and applications.

This section concludes by recognizing the collective impact of these pioneers and visionaries on the field of AI. Their groundbreaking research, innovative ideas, and tireless dedication have shaped the trajectory of AI, propelling it towards a future where intelligent machines play increasingly integral roles in society. As we honor their legacies, we acknowledge their profound influence on shaping the future of technology and society through AI.

Chapter 2: AI Decoded

Artificial intelligence (AI) refers to the simulation of human intelligence in machines that are programmed to think and act like humans. It encompasses a broad range of techniques and technologies aimed at enabling machines to perform tasks that typically require human intelligence, such as problem-solving, decision-making, speech recognition, and language translation.

2.1 Defining Artificial Intelligence

Artificial Intelligence (AI) embodies the pinnacle of technological advancements, simulating human intellect through machines designed to mimic human thoughts and actions. At its core, AI integrates a vast array of techniques and innovations, propelling machines to execute tasks once exclusive to human cognition—ranging from problem-solving and decision-making to speech recognition and language translation.

2.1.1 Essential Characteristics of AI

AI's brilliance shines through its distinct characteristics, each contributing to its ability to replicate and enhance human cognitive functions:

A. Learning

Central to AI's evolution is its capacity for learning. Through the ingestion of data, experiences, and iterative feedback, AI systems continuously refine and elevate their performance. This adaptive learning enables AI to tackle increasingly complex challenges with greater accuracy over time.

B. Reasoning

AI stands out for its reasoning capability. By analyzing data and applying logical frameworks, AI systems can draw informed conclusions and make decisions. This attribute is foundational in scenarios that demand critical thinking and strategic planning.

C. Problem-solving

At the heart of AI's utility is its problem-solving prowess. AI approaches complex issues by deconstructing them into smaller, more manageable segments. Through strategic analysis, AI identifies optimal solutions, often surpassing human efficiency in both speed and accuracy.

D. Perception

AI's ability to perceive and interpret sensory data is a testament to its advanced design. Whether it's recognizing patterns in images, discerning nuances in sound, or understanding the intricacies of written text, AI's perceptual skills enable it to interact with the world in a manner once thought to be uniquely human.

AI's integration into our daily lives is increasingly seamless, significantly enhancing efficiency, creativity, and decision-making processes across various domains. Its development marks a revolutionary step in our journey towards creating machines that not only complement but also augment human capabilities, heralding a new era of innovation and discovery.

2.2 Core Components of AI Systems

Artificial Intelligence (AI) systems are sophisticated constructs, reliant on several foundational components that enable them to mimic human cognitive functions with remarkable efficiency. Each component plays a critical role in the system's ability to learn, reason, solve problems, and perceive the world. Here, we explore the essential elements that constitute the backbone of AI systems:

2.2.1   *Fundamental Elements of AI*

A. Data

Dubbed as the lifeblood of AI, data acts as the starting point from which all AI intelligence flows. It provides the essential raw material needed for the training of AI models, enabling them to derive meaningful insights and make informed predictions. The quality, diversity, and relevance of data directly influence the efficacy and accuracy of AI predictions, underscoring the importance of comprehensive and well-curated datasets.

B. Algorithms

Algorithms are the heart of AI systems, constituting the mathematical and logical frameworks that guide data processing, pattern recognition, and decision-making processes. They range from simple formulas to complex mechanisms tailored for specific tasks like classification, regression, clustering, and reinforcement learning. The choice of algorithm significantly impacts the system's performance, adaptability, and efficiency in addressing varied challenges.

C. Computing Power

The muscle behind AI's processing capabilities lies in its demand for substantial computing power. The ability to sift through vast datasets and perform intricate calculations at speed is pivotal to AI's success. Innovations in hardware, particularly in GPUs (Graphics Processing Units) and TPUs (Tensor Processing Units), have catapulted the processing speed, making real-time analysis and complex model training feasible and more accessible.

D.   Model Training

The process of model training is akin to the educational journey of AI systems, where algorithms learn to perform tasks by being fed data. This stage is crucial for adjusting the model's parameters to reduce errors and enhance accuracy. Through iterative training, models evolve to make precise predictions and decisions, reflecting a refined understanding of the task at hand.

E. *Deployment and Integration*

The culmination of AI development is its deployment and integration into operational environments. Trained models are deployed onto suitable platforms, ranging from cloud-based servers to edge devices, ensuring they operate efficiently in real-world scenarios. Furthermore, integration with existing systems and applications is crucial for harnessing AI's potential, facilitating seamless interaction and value addition across various sectors.

The orchestration of these components into a cohesive system defines the capabilities and effectiveness of AI applications. From revolutionizing industries to enhancing everyday experiences, the strategic assembly and optimization of data, algorithms, computing power, model training, and deployment mechanisms are instrumental in unlocking the transformative power of AI.

2.3 *The Spectrum of AI: From Narrow to General Intelligence*

The realm of Artificial Intelligence (AI) is vast and varied, stretching across a spectrum that delineates the capabilities and potential of AI systems. This spectrum is broadly categorized into two distinct types of AI: Narrow AI and General AI. Each represents a unique level of intelligence and applicability, from specialized functions to the aspiration of mimicking human intellect in its entirety.

2.3.1 *Diverse Categories of AI*

A. *Narrow AI:*

- *Definition and Scope*

Narrow AI, also recognized as weak AI, is specialized in its functionality. It is designed with a focus to excel at a specific task or a set of closely related tasks within a confined domain. The brilliance of narrow AI lies in its precision and efficiency in executing the tasks it is programmed for.

- *Examples and Applications*

The most common manifestations of narrow AI are seen in our daily interactions with technology. Virtual assistants like Siri and Alexa, recommendation engines that curate personalized content on streaming platforms, and sophisticated image recognition systems that categorize and tag photos are quintessential examples of narrow AI at work.

- *Limitations*

Despite its prowess in specific domains, narrow AI is not equipped to venture beyond its programmed capabilities. It does not possess the ability to generalize its learning or understanding to broader contexts, limiting its functionality to its predefined tasks.

B. General AI:

- *Definition and Aspirations*

General AI, or artificial general intelligence (AGI), is the zenith of AI research, representing systems that could emulate human intelligence in its entirety. The vision behind general AI is to create machines that can understand, learn, and apply knowledge across a wide range of tasks, mirroring the cognitive abilities of humans.

- *Theoretical Status*

As of now, general AI remains within the realm of theory and ambition. Achieving a machine with human-level cognitive abilities encompasses immense technical hurdles and ethical considerations. The complexities involved in replicating the nuances of human intelligence, including emotional understanding, creative thinking, and moral judgment, present formidable challenges.

- *Ethical and Safety Concerns*

The pursuit of general AI raises profound ethical questions and safety concerns. Issues such as ensuring the alignment of AI systems with human values, preventing misuse, and managing potential societal impacts are central to the discourse surrounding the development of general AI.

The journey from narrow AI to the aspirational goal of general AI encapsulates the evolutionary path of artificial intelligence. Narrow AI, with its targeted efficacy, serves as the foundation upon which the dream of general AI is built. While narrow AI continues to enhance and transform various sectors of society, the quest for general AI pushes the boundaries of what is technically and ethically possible, aiming to redefine the future of human-machine interaction. This spectrum not only highlights the current achievements and practical applications of AI but also underscores the ambitious, yet uncertain, horizon of achieving a machine intelligence indistinguishable from that of humans.

Chapter Review

2.1 Defining Artificial Intelligence

Key characteristics of AI include:

- Learning: AI systems have the ability to learn from data, experiences, and feedback, improving their performance over time.
- Reasoning: AI systems can analyze information, draw conclusions, and make decisions based on logic and rules.
- Problem-solving: AI systems can solve complex problems by breaking them down into smaller, more manageable tasks and finding optimal solutions.
- Perception: AI systems can perceive and interpret sensory inputs, such as images, sounds, and text, enabling them to interact with the environment.

2.2 Core Components of AI Systems

AI systems typically consist of several core components, including:

- Data: Data is the foundation of AI systems, serving as the raw material from which insights and intelligence are derived. High-quality, relevant data is essential for training AI models and making accurate predictions.
- Algorithms: Algorithms are the mathematical formulas and rules that AI systems use to process data, extract patterns, and make decisions. Different algorithms are suited to different types of tasks, such as classification, regression, clustering, and reinforcement learning.
- Computing Power: AI systems require significant computing power to process large volumes of data and perform complex calculations. Advances in hardware, such as GPUs and TPUs, have greatly accelerated the development and deployment of AI applications.
- Model Training: Model training involves feeding data into AI algorithms to teach them how to perform specific tasks. During training, the algorithms adjust their parameters to minimize errors and optimize performance, resulting in trained models that can make accurate predictions and decisions.
- Deployment and Integration: Once trained, AI models need to be deployed and integrated into real-world systems and applications. This involves deploying the models on appropriate infrastructure, such as cloud servers or edge devices, and integrating them with existing software and hardware.

2.3 The Spectrum of AI: From Narrow to General Intelligence

AI systems can be categorized along a spectrum ranging from narrow to general intelligence:

- Narrow AI: Narrow AI, also known as weak AI, is designed to perform specific tasks or functions within a limited domain. Examples of narrow AI include virtual assistants, recommendation systems, and image recognition algorithms. While narrow AI excels at performing predefined tasks, it lacks the ability to generalize beyond its training data or context.

- General AI: General AI, also known as strong AI or artificial general intelligence (AGI), refers to AI systems that possess human-level intelligence and can perform any intellectual task that a human can. General AI remains a theoretical concept and has not yet been achieved. Developing general AI poses significant technical and ethical challenges, including ensuring safety, ethics, and alignment with human values.

Part II: Technologies Driving AI

Chapter 3: Machine Learning – The Backbone of AI

Machine Learning (ML) stands as a cornerstone in the realm of Artificial Intelligence (AI), enabling systems to learn from data, identify patterns, and make decisions with minimal human intervention. This chapter delves into the intricacies of machine learning, exploring its foundational principles, key algorithms, and the myriad of applications that transform everyday life and industries at large.

3.1 Introduction to Machine Learning

Machine Learning (ML) is a transformative branch of Artificial Intelligence (AI) that fundamentally shifts how software applications improve and evolve with experience. It empowers computers to learn from data, identify patterns, and make decisions without being explicitly programmed for every specific task. This introduction unpacks the essence of machine learning, elucidating its core principles, operational mechanisms, and the categorization that underpins its diverse applications.

3.1.1   *Core Principles and Mechanisms*

A. *Definition and Essence*

Machine learning is a technique that enables machines to automatically learn and adapt from experience. It focuses on the development of computer programs that can access data and use it to learn for themselves. The primary aim is to allow computers to learn automatically without human intervention or assistance and adjust actions accordingly.

B. How Machine Learning Works

The process begins with feeding datasets to algorithms, which then analyze and learn from the data. This learning involves identifying patterns, making predictions, or generating insights, which are then applied to make informed decisions when faced with new, unseen data. Over time, as more data is processed, the algorithm becomes increasingly accurate in its predictions or decisions.

C. Learning from Data

The essence of machine learning lies in its ability to transform data into insights. Data, in various forms (e.g., images, text, numbers), is the fuel for machine learning models. These models sift through data, learning from its structure and intricacies, enabling the extraction of valuable information that can guide decision-making processes.

3.1.2   Types of Machine Learning

Machine learning can be categorized into three primary types based on the nature of the learning signal or feedback available to a learning system:

A. Supervised Learning

This type involves learning a function that maps an input to an output based on example input-output pairs. It infers a function from labeled training data consisting of a set of training examples. Each example is a pair consisting of an input object (typically a vector) and the desired output value (also called the supervisory signal).

B. Unsupervised Learning

In unsupervised learning, the system tries to learn without any supervision. The system doesn't have labelled data, meaning it explores the data and can automatically find structure and patterns. Common unsupervised learning techniques include clustering and association.

C. Reinforcement Learning

This type is different from supervised and unsupervised learning. In reinforcement learning, an algorithm learns to perform an action from experience. Reinforcement learning is about taking suitable action to maximize reward in a particular situation. It is employed by various software and machines to find the best possible behavior or path it should take in a specific context.

3.1.3 Operational Mechanisms

A. Model Training

Involves adjusting the model's parameters to minimize the difference between the predicted output and the actual output. This process, often iterative, improves the model's performance over time.

B. Prediction and Decision-Making

Once trained, the model can make predictions or decisions when exposed to new data. This capability is the hallmark of machine learning, enabling applications to deliver personalized experiences and make intelligent choices.

C. Continuous Learning

A significant advantage of machine learning models is their ability to continuously learn and adapt. As they are exposed to new data, they can update their understanding and improve their predictions and decisions.

Machine learning stands as a pillar of modern AI, offering a framework for computers to evolve and improve from experience. Its capacity to learn from data, identify patterns, and make informed decisions without explicit programming is revolutionizing how we interact with technology, paving the way for innovations across various fields and industries.

3.2 Key Machine Learning Algorithms

Machine learning algorithms are the backbone of AI applications, enabling systems to learn from data, make predictions, and improve over time. These algorithms can be broadly categorized based on their learning style and function: supervised learning, unsupervised learning, and reinforcement learning. Within these categories, several key algorithms stand out for their versatility, efficiency, and widespread application. This section delves into the core algorithms that form the foundation of machine learning.

3.2.1 _Supervised Learning Algorithms_

A. Linear Regression:

-   Description: A fundamental algorithm used for predicting a continuous variable. It establishes a relationship between a dependent variable (target) and one or more independent variables (predictors) by fitting a linear equation to observed data.
-   Applications: Real estate for predicting house prices, finance for forecasting stock prices, and more.

B. Logistic Regression:

-   Description: Despite its name, it's a classification algorithm used to estimate discrete values (binary outcomes like 0/1, yes/no) based on a given set of independent variables.
-   Applications: Email spam detection, online transaction fraud detection, and medical diagnoses.

C. Decision Trees:

-   Description: A tree-like model of decisions and their possible consequences. It splits a dataset into smaller subsets while simultaneously developing an associated decision tree.
-   Applications: Customer segmentation, business decision making, and diagnosing medical conditions.

D. Random Forest:

- Description: An ensemble method that operates by constructing multiple decision trees at training time and outputting the class that is the mode of the classes (classification) or mean prediction (regression) of the individual trees.
- Applications: Banking for credit risk assessment, retail for inventory prediction, and medicine for identifying disease patterns.

3.2.2 *Unsupervised Learning Algorithms*

A.K-Means Clustering:

- Description: A method to partition n observations into k clusters in which each observation belongs to the cluster with the nearest mean.
- Applications: Market segmentation, document clustering, and image segmentation.

B.Principal Component Analysis (PCA):

- Description: A technique used to emphasize variation and bring out strong patterns in a dataset, reducing its dimensions without losing much information.
- Applications: Genetics for identifying genetic markers, finance for risk management models, and image compression.

3.2.3 *Reinforcement Learning Algorithms*

A. Q-Learning:

- Description: A model-free reinforcement learning algorithm that learns the quality of actions, telling an agent what action to take under what circumstances.
- Applications: Robotics for optimizing the robot's behavior, gaming for developing strategies, and autonomous vehicles for decision-making processes.

B. Deep Q-Networks (DQN):

- Description: Combines Q-learning with deep neural networks at scale, learning successful policies directly from high-dimensional sensory inputs.
- Applications: Playing and mastering complex video games, robotic controls, and optimizing logistics.

3.2.4   *Specialized Algorithms*

A. Convolutional Neural Networks (CNNs):

- Description: A class of deep neural networks, most commonly applied to analyzing visual imagery. They use a mathematical operation called convolution which allows the network to focus on specific aspects of an input.
- Applications: Image and video recognition, image classification, and medical image analysis.

B. Recurrent Neural Networks (RNNs):

- Description: A type of neural network where connections between nodes form a directed graph along a temporal sequence, allowing it to exhibit temporal dynamic behavior.
- Applications: Language modeling, speech recognition, and text generation.

These key machine learning algorithms are the tools that power a vast range of AI applications, transforming data into actionable insights and predictive power across industries. From simple linear models that predict continuous values to complex neural networks that decipher images and language, the diversity and adaptability of these algorithms underscore the dynamism and potential of machine learning in tackling some of today's most challenging problems.

3.3 Real-world Applications of Machine Learning

Machine Learning (ML) has transcended research laboratories and theoretical discussions, embedding itself into the fabric of our everyday lives and the operational frameworks of industries worldwide. Its applications are as diverse as they are transformative, leveraging data to solve complex problems, enhance decision-making, and create innovative services and products. This section explores the breadth of machine learning applications, highlighting how they impact various sectors and aspects of daily life.

3.3.1 *Transformative Sectors*

A.Healthcare:

- *Disease Diagnosis and Imaging*

ML algorithms analyze medical images (MRI, CT scans) with high precision, assisting in early and accurate disease diagnosis, including cancer, Alzheimer's, and cardiovascular diseases.

- *Drug Discovery and Development*

Speeds up research cycles, identifying potential therapeutic candidates in lesser time and at reduced costs compared to traditional methods.

B.Finance:

- *Fraud Detection*

Machine learning models are trained to recognize patterns indicative of fraudulent transactions, significantly reducing the incidence of financial fraud.

-   *Algorithmic Trading*

ML algorithms can predict market changes and execute trades at optimal times, maximizing profits and minimizing risks.

C. *Automotive and Transportation:*

-   *Autonomous Vehicles*

Self-driving cars use machine learning to process sensor data, enabling them to navigate safely in complex environments.

-   *Traffic Management*

ML helps in analyzing traffic patterns to optimize traffic flow and reduce congestion.

D. *Retail and E-Commerce:*

-   *Personalized Shopping Experiences*

Recommender systems use ML to analyze browsing and purchase history, offering personalized product recommendations to users.

-   *Inventory Management*

Predictive analytics optimize stock levels and distribution, reducing costs and improving efficiency.

E. *Entertainment and Media:*

-   *Content Recommendation*

Platforms like Netflix and Spotify use machine learning to suggest movies, TV shows, and music tailored to the user's preferences.

-   *Video Games*

ML enhances non-player character (NPC) behavior, making them more realistic and responsive to player actions.

3.3.2 *Impactful Applications*

A. Natural Language Processing (NLP):

- *Voice Assistants and Chatbots*

Siri, Alexa, and Google Assistant use NLP to understand and respond to user queries with natural language, improving user experience and accessibility.

- *Translation Services*

Tools like Google Translate use ML to provide real-time, accurate translations across numerous languages, bridging communication gaps.

B. Agriculture:

- *Crop and Soil Monitoring*

Machine learning models predict crop health and productivity, advising farmers on optimal planting strategies and resource allocation.

- *Precision Farming*

Automates and optimizes farming practices, using drones and sensors to monitor crop health, improving yields and reducing environmental impact.

C. Education:

- *Personalized Learning*

Adaptive learning platforms use ML to tailor educational content to the student's learning pace and style, enhancing engagement and comprehension.

- Automated Grading and Feedback

Reduces teachers' workload by automating grading of multiple-choice and fill-in-the-blank tests, providing instant feedback to students.

D. Environmental Protection:

- Climate Change Analysis

Machine learning algorithms analyze climate data to predict changes, helping in formulating strategies to mitigate adverse effects.

- Wildlife Conservation

ML-powered drones and camera traps monitor endangered species, collecting data that helps in conservation efforts.

Machine Learning's versatility and power to process and analyze vast datasets have revolutionized how we approach challenges and opportunities across various fields. From enhancing healthcare outcomes and advancing financial security to driving innovations in entertainment and beyond, ML's real-world applications underscore its role as a pivotal force in shaping the future, making processes more efficient, insights more accessible, and technologies more adaptive and intelligent.

Chapter Review

3.1 Introduction to Machine Learning

- Defining Machine Learning: At its core, machine learning is a subset of AI that empowers computers to learn from and interpret data without being explicitly programmed for every task. Through exposure to data, machine learning algorithms can adjust and improve their performance, making them more efficient and accurate over time.

- How It Works: Machine learning processes involve feeding data into algorithms, which then analyze and learn from the data. This learning phase allows the model to identify patterns or structures within the data, enabling it to make predictions or decisions based on its training. As new data is introduced, these models adapt, enhancing their accuracy and relevance.
- Types of Machine Learning: The field is broadly categorized into supervised learning, where models learn from labeled data; unsupervised learning, where models infer patterns from unlabeled data; and reinforcement learning, where models learn through trial and error to make sequences of decisions.

3.2 Key Machine Learning Algorithms

- Linear Regression: Utilized for predicting a continuous value. For example, predicting the price of a house based on its features is a typical application of linear regression.
- Decision Trees: These are versatile algorithms that can be used for classification and regression tasks. They work by breaking down a dataset into smaller subsets while at the same time an associated decision tree is incrementally developed.
- Clustering Algorithms (e.g., K-Means): Used in unsupervised learning to group unlabelled data into clusters based on similarity metrics. This is commonly used in market segmentation, image compression, and more.
- Neural Networks: Inspired by the human brain's architecture, neural networks are a complex series of algorithms that have led to significant advancements in deep learning. They are particularly effective in processing images, speech, and complex patterns.
- Reinforcement Learning (e.g., Q-Learning): This type of learning uses agents that interact with an environment to achieve a goal or maximize some notion of cumulative reward. It has been famously applied in game-playing AI and robotics.

3.3 Real-world Applications of Machine Learning

- Healthcare: Machine learning algorithms are revolutionizing healthcare by improving diagnostic accuracy, personalizing treatment plans, and predicting patient outcomes. For instance,

ML models can analyze medical images to detect diseases at early stages.
- Finance: In the finance sector, machine learning is employed for algorithmic trading, fraud detection, and risk management, enhancing decision-making and operational efficiency.
- Autonomous Vehicles: Self-driving cars leverage machine learning to interpret sensor data, navigate roads, and make driving decisions, pushing the envelope of what's possible in transportation.
- Recommendation Systems: Platforms like Netflix and Amazon use machine learning to analyze user behavior and preferences, offering personalized content or product recommendations to enhance user experience.
- Natural Language Processing (NLP): Machine learning algorithms are at the heart of NLP applications, enabling computers to understand, interpret, and generate human language. Applications include voice-activated assistants, translation services, and sentiment analysis.

Machine learning is reshaping the world, driving innovations across sectors by providing systems the ability to automatically learn and improve from experience. Its versatility and power in processing vast amounts of data hold the key to solving some of the most complex challenges of our time, marking a new era in the advancement of artificial intelligence.

Chapter 4: Deep Learning – AI's Deep Mind

Deep learning, a pivotal innovation in artificial intelligence, harnesses the computational power of neural networks to interpret complex data structures, mimicking the intricate processes of the human brain. This chapter delves into the essence of deep learning, elucidates the architectural complexities of neural networks, and explores the transformative breakthroughs enabled by this technology.

4.1 Unraveling Deep Learning

Deep learning is a transformative force at the intersection of data science, artificial intelligence (AI), and machine learning (ML), providing sophisticated tools for predictive analysis and intelligent decision-making. This section explores the conceptual underpinnings and learning mechanisms that make deep learning a powerful subset of AI.

4.1.1 Conceptual Foundations

Deep learning is predicated on the concept of artificial neural networks (ANNs), which are inspired by the biological neural networks that constitute animal brains. This approach to AI seeks to emulate the way humans learn from their environment, creating machines capable of understanding complex patterns and making decisions with little human intervention.

A. Biological Inspiration

Just as neurons in the human brain transmit signals through a complex network, ANNs consist of interconnected units or nodes that process data and communicate information across various layers.

B. Data Processing Hierarchy

Deep learning models structure data processing in layers, forming a hierarchy that allows for the abstraction of features from simple to increasingly complex. This hierarchical structure enables the model to learn from vast amounts of data, extracting intricate patterns that are not immediately apparent.

4.1.2 *Mechanisms of Learning*

The essence of deep learning lies in its ability to learn and improve from experience. This learning occurs through a meticulously structured process involving the adjustment of the neural network's synaptic weights, a task accomplished through backpropagation and optimization algorithms.

A. Backpropagation

At the heart of deep learning's learning process is backpropagation. This algorithm plays a pivotal role in training ANNs by efficiently calculating the gradient of the loss function (a measure of prediction error) and propagating this information back through the network to adjust the weights. The goal is to minimize the loss function, thereby improving the model's accuracy over time.

B. Optimization Algorithms

Complementing backpropagation, various optimization algorithms are employed to find the most effective weight adjustments to reduce the loss function. Techniques such as Stochastic Gradient Descent (SGD), Adam, and RMSprop vary in their approach to navigating the weight space but share the common goal of enhancing the learning speed and performance of the neural network.

C. Regularization and Dropout

To prevent overfitting—a scenario where the model learns the training data too well but performs poorly on new data—deep learning utilizes techniques like regularization and dropout. Regularization adds a penalty on larger weights to simplify the model, whereas dropout randomly ignores a subset of neurons during training, encouraging the network to develop redundant pathways and improve generalization.

D.   *Feature Extraction and Representation Learning*

Deep learning automates the feature extraction process, distinguishing it from traditional machine learning approaches. Instead of relying on hand-engineered features, deep learning models are capable of learning representations from raw data, making them exceptionally adept at handling complex, high-dimensional datasets across various domains.

Deep learning, through its advanced neural networks and sophisticated learning mechanisms, heralds a new era in artificial intelligence. It offers the promise of machines that can learn, adapt, and make decisions with a level of complexity and nuance that approaches human intelligence, transforming industries and enabling new applications that were once considered the realm of science fiction.

4.2 *Architecture of Neural Networks*

The architecture of neural networks reflects the depth and complexity of deep learning models, designed to navigate the intricacies of vast and varied datasets. This section delves into the foundational structure of neural networks, explores the diversity of network architectures tailored to specific tasks, and highlights advanced techniques that enhance model performance.

4.2.1   *Structural Overview*

Neural networks are intricate systems composed of multiple layers of neurons, or nodes, each playing a distinct role in the data processing pipeline. This structured arrangement is fundamental to the network's ability to learn and model complex patterns.

A. Layered Architecture

At its most basic, a neural network includes an input layer, one or more hidden layers, and an output layer. The input layer receives the data, the hidden layers process the data through various computational functions, and the output layer produces the final decision or prediction.

B. Hidden Layers

The hidden layers are where the majority of computation takes place. These layers can be numerous and varied, allowing the network to abstract and build complex representations of the input data. The depth and breadth of these layers contribute to the network's "deep" learning capability.

4.2.2 Diverse Architectures

The architecture of neural networks has evolved, branching into specialized structures that cater to different types of data and learning tasks. Each architecture has unique characteristics that make it suited for specific applications.

A. Convolutional Neural Networks (CNNs)

CNNs are optimized for processing data with a grid-like topology, such as images. Through the use of convolutional layers, CNNs are able to capture spatial hierarchies in the data, making them highly effective for tasks that require the recognition of visual patterns.

B. Recurrent Neural Networks (RNNs)

RNNs are designed to handle sequential data, such as text or time series. They achieve this by maintaining a form of memory that allows them to use information from previous inputs to inform current and future outputs. This characteristic makes RNNs ideal for tasks where context and order matter.

C. Transformers

Transformers represent a significant advancement over traditional RNNs by introducing self-attention mechanisms. These mechanisms allow the model to weigh the importance of different parts of the input data relative to each other, enabling parallel processing of sequences and significantly improving efficiency and performance in tasks like language translation and text generation.

4.2.3   Advanced Techniques

The effectiveness of neural networks is further enhanced by a suite of advanced techniques that optimize their learning process and improve generalization to unseen data.

A. Dropout

A regularization technique that mitigates the risk of overfitting by randomly "dropping out" a subset of neurons during training. This forces the network to learn more robust features that are not reliant on any single neuron.

B. Normalization

Techniques like batch normalization standardize the inputs to each layer within the network, improving the stability and speed of the learning process. This normalization helps in accelerating convergence and reducing the sensitivity to network initialization.

C. Optimization Algorithms

The choice of optimization algorithm can have a profound impact on the training efficiency and outcome of neural networks. Algorithms such as Adam and RMSprop adapt the learning rate during training, allowing for more efficient navigation of the weight space and faster convergence.

The architecture of neural networks, with its foundational structures, specialized forms, and advanced techniques, underscores the adaptability and sophistication of deep learning models. These architectural innovations enable neural networks to tackle a broad spectrum of challenges across various domains, from image and speech recognition to natural language understanding and beyond.

4.3 Breakthroughs Enabled by Deep Learning

Deep learning has been instrumental in driving significant advancements across various fields, demonstrating the vast capabilities of artificial intelligence. This section explores the pivotal breakthroughs catalyzed by deep learning, highlighting its impact on perception, language processing, autonomous navigation, healthcare, and strategic game playing.

4.3.1 *Revolution in Perception*

Deep learning has dramatically enhanced the capabilities of machines in understanding and interpreting visual and auditory information, leading to groundbreaking applications.

A. *Image Recognition*

The deployment of Convolutional Neural Networks (CNNs) has vastly improved the accuracy of image recognition systems, enabling applications ranging from facial recognition technology in security systems to medical image analysis for disease detection.

B. *Speech Recognition*

Advancements in deep learning have significantly improved speech recognition systems. This has facilitated the development of responsive and accurate personal assistants, transformed customer service with speech-to-text services, and improved accessibility for people with disabilities.

4.3.2 *Mastery of Language*

The application of deep learning in natural language processing (NLP) has led to substantial improvements in understanding, translating, and generating human language.

A. Language Translation

Deep learning models, particularly those based on the Transformer architecture, have revolutionized machine translation, achieving near-human levels of accuracy and fluency in real-time language translation services.

B. Chatbots and Virtual Assistants

Enhanced NLP capabilities have enabled the creation of sophisticated chatbots and virtual assistants that understand and generate natural language, providing users with more intuitive and helpful interactions.

4.3.3 *Autonomous Navigation*

Deep learning has paved the way for significant advancements in autonomous vehicle technology, enhancing safety and efficiency in transportation.

A. Self-Driving Cars

By processing data from sensors and cameras in real-time, deep learning algorithms allow autonomous vehicles to make informed decisions, navigate complex environments, and recognize obstacles, leading to safer roads and reduced human error.

4.3.4 *Healthcare Innovations*

In healthcare, deep learning models are transforming diagnostics, treatment planning, and patient care, making significant strides in personalized medicine.

A. *Diagnostic Accuracy*

Deep learning algorithms have achieved remarkable success in diagnosing diseases from medical images, often with greater accuracy than human experts, especially in areas like cancer detection and retinal diseases.

B. *Predictive Analytics*

Utilizing vast datasets, deep learning models can predict disease progression and outcomes, enabling healthcare providers to tailor treatment plans to individual patients, improving efficacy and patient care.

4.3.5 *Game-Changing Strategies*

Deep learning has also demonstrated its prowess in complex strategic games, showcasing the potential for AI in problem-solving and strategic planning.

- *AlphaGo and Beyond*

The success of AI systems like AlphaGo, which defeated world champions in the complex game of Go, illustrates the strategic depth and learning capabilities of deep learning models. This has implications for solving complex problems in logistics, finance, and beyond.

Deep learning continues to drive the evolution of artificial intelligence, pushing the boundaries of what machines can learn and achieve. Its impact spans across industries, from transforming user interaction and enhancing safety in autonomous systems to revolutionizing healthcare and redefining strategic decision-making. As deep learning models become increasingly sophisticated, their potential to innovate and improve human life seems boundless, heralding a future where AI plays a central role in addressing some of the world's most challenging problems.

Chapter Review

4.1 Unraveling Deep Learning

Deep learning stands at the confluence of data science, artificial intelligence, and machine learning, offering a profound mechanism for predictive analysis and decision-making.

- 4.1.1 Conceptual Foundations: At its heart, deep learning involves training artificial neural networks on a vast array of data. These networks are designed to simulate the neural structure of the human brain, enabling machines to learn from experiences and understand the world in a hierarchy of complexity.
- 4.1.2 Mechanisms of Learning: The learning process within these networks occurs through the adjustment of synaptic weights, which are fine-tuned during training. This adjustment is facilitated by backpropagation, a cornerstone algorithm that calculates and distributes errors back through the network, allowing for efficient learning.

4.2 Architecture of Neural Networks

The architecture of neural networks is a testament to the flexibility and adaptability of deep learning models, tailored to meet the demands of diverse datasets and problem statements.

C. 4.2.1 Structural Overview: Neural networks are composed of layers of interconnected nodes or neurons, including input, hidden, and output layers. The hidden layers, which can be deep and numerous, are where the bulk of processing occurs, enabling the network to capture complex patterns and relationships in the data.
- 4.2.2 Diverse Architectures: The landscape of neural networks is rich and varied, encompassing:
    - Convolutional Neural Networks (CNNs): Specialized for spatial data processing, making them ideal for image and video recognition tasks.
    - Recurrent Neural Networks (RNNs): Suited for sequential data, such as time series analysis or natural

language processing, due to their memory of previous inputs.

- o Transformers: A revolutionary model that has outpaced RNNs in language understanding tasks, leveraging self-attention mechanisms to process sequences of data in parallel.
- 4.2.3 Advanced Techniques: Enhancements such as dropout, normalization, and sophisticated optimization algorithms (e.g., Adam) further optimize the training process, bolstering the network's ability to learn efficiently and effectively.

4.3 Breakthroughs Enabled by Deep Learning

Deep learning has catalyzed a series of breakthroughs across various domains, pushing the boundaries of what machines can learn and accomplish.

- 4.3.1 Revolution in Perception: The accuracy of image and speech recognition systems has seen unprecedented improvements, facilitating advancements in autonomous vehicles, personal assistants, and surveillance systems.
- 4.3.2 Mastery of Language: In the realm of natural language processing, deep learning has given rise to models that understand, translate, and generate human language with remarkable proficiency, enabling real-time translation services, sophisticated chatbots, and more.
- 4.3.3 Autonomous Navigation: The application of deep learning in autonomous vehicles has led to safer and more efficient navigation systems, capable of real-time decision-making in complex, unpredictable environments.
- 4.3.4 Healthcare Innovations: Deep learning models are revolutionizing healthcare by providing more accurate diagnoses, predicting patient outcomes, and personalizing treatment plans, thereby enhancing the quality and effectiveness of medical care.
- 4.3.5 Game-Changing Strategies: The victory of AI systems like AlphaGo over human champions in strategy games underscores the strategic depth and intuition that deep learning models can achieve, heralding new applications in complex problem-solving and decision-making.

Deep learning, with its robust, flexible architectures and wide-ranging applications, continues to be a driving force in the evolution of artificial intelligence, shaping the future of technology and its integration into every aspect of human life.

Chapter 5: Other AI Technologies

While deep learning has been a pivotal force in the advancement of artificial intelligence (AI), several other AI technologies have also played crucial roles in shaping the current landscape of innovation. These technologies, ranging from natural language processing to augmented and virtual reality, have expanded the capabilities of AI systems, enabling them to interact with the world and humans in more nuanced and impactful ways.

5.1 Natural Language Processing (NLP)

Natural Language Processing (NLP) represents a dynamic and essential field at the confluence of artificial intelligence (AI) and linguistics, dedicated to bridging the gap between human language and computer understanding. This technology enables machines to parse, comprehend, and generate human language in a way that is both meaningful and contextually relevant, transforming our interactions with digital systems.

5.1.1 Key Areas of NLP

A. Language Understanding

- *Semantic Analysis*

NLP systems analyze the meaning behind words in text and speech, understanding context, nuances, and the intent of the language used. This understanding is crucial for applications requiring a deep comprehension of human input, such as answering questions accurately or interpreting commands correctly.

- *Syntactic Parsing*

Beyond semantics, NLP involves dissecting sentences to understand grammatical structure, enabling machines to grasp the relationship between words and phrases, thus enhancing comprehension accuracy.

B. Language Generation

- *Automated Content Creation*

Leveraging AI to produce text that resembles human-written content, NLP is behind the generation of news articles, reports, and even creative writing, streamlining content creation processes across various sectors.

- *Interactive Conversations*

Through NLP, virtual assistants and chatbots can engage in naturalistic dialogues with users, providing assistance, information, or entertainment based on the conversation's context and flow.

C. Speech Recognition and Generation

- *Voice-Activated Control*

Transforming vocal commands into actionable input, speech-to-text technology allows users to interact with devices hands-free, enhancing accessibility and convenience.

- *Text-to-Speech (TTS)*

TTS systems convert written text into spoken word, aiding in accessibility for visually impaired individuals and creating more dynamic user experiences in applications ranging from navigation to audiobook reading.

5.1.2 *Impact and Applications*

A. Enhanced Communication

- *Breaking Language Barriers*

NLP technologies such as real-time translation services have made it easier for people to communicate across language divides, fostering global collaboration and understanding.

- *Accessibility Improvements*

By enabling more natural interactions with technology through voice and text, NLP has made digital information and services more accessible to a wider range of users, including those with disabilities.

B. *Content Analysis and Generation*

- *Efficient Information Processing*

NLP tools can quickly analyze large volumes of text to extract insights, trends, and summaries, making it invaluable in fields like research, journalism, and business intelligence.

- *Creative Content Generation*

AI-driven content generation tools are reshaping the creative landscape, providing new ways to produce written content, from marketing copy to personalized stories, at scale and with increased efficiency.

5.1.3   *Conclusion*

Natural Language Processing stands as a pillar of modern AI, enabling machines to understand and generate human language in ways that are increasingly sophisticated and impactful. By enhancing communication, breaking down language barriers, and automating content-related tasks, NLP technologies are not only advancing our interaction with machines but also transforming industries and opening up new possibilities for accessibility and creativity. As NLP continues to evolve, its role in shaping the future of technology and society is both significant and far-reaching, promising even greater advancements and applications in the years to come.

5.2 Robotics and Autonomous Systems

Robotics and autonomous systems represent a transformative technological domain, where the synergy of AI, mechanical engineering, and electronic engineering brings forth machines capable of performing complex tasks independently. This integration allows robots to navigate diverse environments, make decisions, and execute actions without direct human oversight, marking a significant leap in the capabilities of machines to assist, augment, and sometimes replace human effort in various contexts.

5.2.1   *Key Components*

A. Sensors and Actuators

- *Perception and Interaction*

Sensors imbue robots with the ability to perceive their surroundings through inputs like light, sound, pressure, and temperature. Actuators, on the other hand, are the muscles of robots, converting energy into motion. Together, they allow robots to interact with their environment in a meaningful way.

- *Integration with AI*

The data gathered by sensors serve as the foundation for AI-based analysis, enabling robots to understand and adapt to their environment. Actuators respond under the guidance of AI-driven decisions, allowing for precise and intelligent manipulation and movement.

B. Machine Learning and Computer Vision

- *Adaptive Learning*

Machine learning algorithms enable robots to improve their performance over time based on experience. By analyzing data from past actions and their outcomes, these systems refine their decision-making processes, enhancing their ability to execute tasks efficiently and accurately.

- *Environmental Recognition*

Computer vision allows robots to interpret visual information from their surroundings. This capability is crucial for tasks that require object recognition, spatial navigation, and interaction with people and other objects in real-time.

5.2.2 *Impact and Applications*

A. *Manufacturing and Logistics*

- *Production Efficiency*

In manufacturing, robots equipped with AI and advanced sensors perform precise and repetitive tasks at speeds and consistency unmatched by human labor. This shift has led to significant improvements in productivity, quality control, and operational efficiency.

- *Warehouse Automation*

Autonomous robots in logistics streamline inventory management, sorting, and transport tasks within warehouses, reducing manual labor requirements and enhancing supply chain efficiency.

B. *Healthcare Robotics*

- *Surgical Precision*

Robotic systems in healthcare, particularly in surgery, offer unparalleled precision, reducing the risk of complications and improving patient outcomes. These systems enable surgeons to perform complex procedures with minimally invasive techniques, leading to quicker recovery times.

- *Rehabilitation and Support*

Robotics also plays a crucial role in rehabilitation, providing adaptive support to individuals recovering from injuries or dealing with mobility challenges. These systems offer personalized therapy sessions, track progress, and adjust treatments as needed, supporting a more effective recovery process.

5.2.3 *Conclusion*

Robotics and autonomous systems are at the forefront of technological innovation, blending AI's analytical prowess with mechanical and electronic ingenuity to create machines that extend human capabilities. Their impact is profoundly felt across sectors, from manufacturing and logistics to healthcare, where they bring about efficiency, safety, and new levels of precision and care. As these technologies continue to evolve, their integration into society will deepen, reshaping our approach to work, healthcare, and daily life, offering glimpses into a future where human and machine collaboration opens up unprecedented possibilities.

5.3 Augmented and Virtual Reality in AI

Augmented Reality (AR) and Virtual Reality (VR) stand as pivotal innovations at the intersection of digital and physical realms, significantly enhanced by artificial intelligence (AI). These technologies not only augment our perception of reality but also create new dimensions of interaction and experience. By leveraging AI, AR and VR are pushed beyond mere display technologies, evolving into intelligent, context-aware systems that respond dynamically to user input and environmental cues.

5.3.1 *Key Aspects*

A. *Immersive Experiences*

- *AR for Enhanced Reality*

Augmented Reality overlays digital information—images, videos, 3D models—onto the real world, enhancing users' perception and interaction with their environment. Through smartphones, tablets, or specialized AR glasses, users can see additional content superimposed onto the physical world, blending digital and physical spaces seamlessly.

- *VR for Total Immersion*

Virtual Reality creates fully immersive digital environments that replace the user's real-world surroundings. Through VR headsets, users are transported into meticulously crafted virtual spaces, from digital recreations of real-world locations to entirely fantastical realms, enabling deep engagement and a profound sense of presence.

B.   *Intelligent Interaction*

- *Context-Aware Enhancements*

AI empowers AR and VR to become context-aware, adjusting content and interactions based on the user's environment, behavior, and preferences. This adaptability enhances the relevance and impact of the experiences, making them more engaging and effective.

- *Real-Time Personalization*

By analyzing data from sensors and user inputs, AI algorithms personalize the AR/VR experiences in real-time, tailoring them to meet individual needs and preferences. This personalization can significantly improve learning outcomes, user satisfaction, and the overall efficacy of the technologies.

5.3.2   *Impact and Applications*

A.   *Education and Training*

- *Simulated Learning Environments*

AR and VR offer immersive learning experiences that simulate real-world scenarios, enabling students and professionals to practice skills, explore complex concepts, and conduct experiments in a safe, controlled environment. These technologies are particularly impactful in medical training, engineering, and history education, providing hands-on experience without real-world risks.

- *Enhanced Engagement*

By making learning interactive and engaging, AR and VR can improve motivation and retention rates, offering a dynamic alternative to traditional educational methods.

B. *Retail and Marketing*

- *Virtual Showrooms and Try-Ons*

Retailers leverage AR and VR to create virtual showrooms and try-on experiences, allowing customers to visualize products in their own space or on their person. This innovative approach reduces the barriers to purchase for online shopping, providing a more informative and interactive buying experience.

- *Interactive Advertising*

In marketing, these technologies offer novel ways to engage consumers, from immersive brand experiences to interactive advertisements that capture the audience's attention and imagination in unprecedented ways.

5.3.3 *Conclusion*

The integration of AR and VR with AI represents a significant leap forward in how we interact with digital content and the world around us. These technologies offer immersive, personalized experiences that have the potential to transform education, retail, marketing, and many other sectors. As AR and VR continue to evolve, their fusion with AI will undoubtedly lead to even more innovative applications, reshaping our digital and physical worlds in profound ways. The future promises not just advancements in how we view reality, but in how we interact, learn, and engage with it, marking a new era of experiential technology.

Chapter Review

5.1 Natural Language Processing (NLP)

Natural Language Processing (NLP) stands at the intersection of AI and linguistics, focusing on the interaction between computers and humans through natural language. It encompasses a broad range of functionalities, from understanding human speech to generating natural-sounding text.

Key Areas of NLP:

- Language Understanding: Involves parsing and semantic analysis of text, enabling AI systems to understand the meaning and context of spoken or written language.
- Language Generation: AI's ability to produce text that mimics human language, used in chatbots, virtual assistants, and content creation tools.
- Speech Recognition and Generation: Converts spoken language into text (speech-to-text) and vice versa (text-to-speech), enhancing the accessibility and usability of technology across various applications.

Impact and Applications:

- Enhanced Communication: NLP has revolutionized the way we interact with technology, making it possible to communicate with machines in our natural language.
- Content Analysis and Generation: From summarizing articles to generating reports, NLP tools have automated and improved the efficiency of content-related tasks.

5.2 Robotics and Autonomous Systems

Robotics and autonomous systems refer to the design, construction, and operation of robots that perform tasks without human intervention. These systems combine AI with mechanical and electronic engineering to create machines capable of navigating and understanding their environment.

Key Components:

- Sensors and Actuators: Equip robots with the ability to perceive their surroundings and move or manipulate objects.
- Machine Learning and Computer Vision: Enable robots to learn from their experiences, recognize objects, and make decisions based on their perceptions.

Impact and Applications:

- Manufacturing and Logistics: Robots have transformed production lines and warehouses, increasing efficiency and safety.
- Healthcare Robotics: From surgical assistants to rehabilitation robots, these systems are enhancing patient care and treatment outcomes.

5.3 Augmented and Virtual Reality in AI

Augmented Reality (AR) and Virtual Reality (VR) technologies enrich the real world with digital information and media, or create entirely immersive environments, respectively. When combined with AI, these technologies offer enriched, interactive experiences that can adapt and respond to user inputs.

Key Aspects:

- Immersive Experiences: AR and VR create engaging environments for entertainment, education, and training, providing users with realistic simulations or enhanced real-world experiences.
- Intelligent Interaction: AI algorithms analyze user interactions and environmental data to tailor the AR/VR experiences, making them more relevant and personalized.

Impact and Applications:

- Education and Training: AR and VR are used for immersive learning experiences, from historical simulations to medical training, offering hands-on practice without real-world risks.

- Retail and Marketing: These technologies allow consumers to visualize products in their own space before purchasing, transforming the shopping experience.

The convergence of these AI technologies—NLP, robotics, and AR/VR—with deep learning and other machine learning methods, is driving the next wave of innovation. Each area not only stands on its own in terms of contributions to our capabilities and understanding but also intersects with others to create novel applications and solutions. As AI continues to evolve, these technologies will play integral roles in shaping a future where AI is seamlessly integrated into every aspect of human life, offering enhanced efficiencies, unprecedented experiences, and deeper insights.

Part III: AI in Action

Chapter 6: AI in Everyday Life

The integration of Artificial Intelligence (AI) into everyday life has transformed mundane tasks, revolutionized entertainment, and even reshaped how we think about mobility and transportation. This chapter explores the pervasive impact of AI in personal and societal domains, highlighting key areas where AI not only enhances efficiency and convenience but also opens new avenues for interaction and engagement.

6.1 Personal Assistants and Smart Homes

6.1.1 Personal Assistants: Revolutionizing Interaction and Convenience

A. Voice-Activated Assistance

AI personal assistants like Amazon Alexa, Google Assistant, and Apple Siri have become household staples, enabling users to perform a wide array of tasks using voice commands. From setting alarms and reminders to fetching news and controlling smart home devices, these assistants have made technology more accessible and interactive.

B. Adaptive Learning and Personalization

These systems utilize advanced machine learning algorithms to adapt to individual user preferences and routines, offering personalized services. Whether it's recommending music based on past choices or optimizing daily schedules, AI assistants continually learn from interactions to enhance user experience.

6.1.2 _Smart Homes: Automating and Enhancing Living Spaces_

A. _Integrated Home Ecosystems_

Smart homes leverage AI to create interconnected systems where devices such as thermostats, lighting, security cameras, and appliances communicate and operate synergistically. This interconnectedness enables automated routines that adjust to the homeowners' lifestyle, promoting energy efficiency and convenience.

B. _Predictive Automation and Control_

Beyond mere automation, AI in smart homes analyzes patterns in user behavior to predict needs, making proactive adjustments. For example, a smart thermostat can learn when the house is typically occupied and adjust the temperature accordingly for optimal comfort and energy savings.

C. _Security and Surveillance_

AI enhances home security systems with features like facial recognition and unusual activity detection, offering homeowners peace of mind. By distinguishing between known occupants and strangers, these systems provide accurate alerts and reduce false alarms.

6.1.3 _Future Directions: Envisioning Next-Generation Smart Living_

A. _Towards More Intuitive Homes_

The future of AI in personal assistants and smart homes points towards even more intuitive and autonomous living environments. This includes advanced natural language understanding for smoother interactions and the integration of AI in virtually all home devices, from kitchen appliances to entertainment systems.

B. Ethical and Privacy Implications

As AI technologies become more embedded in our daily lives, addressing privacy and ethical considerations is paramount. Ensuring data security, protecting user privacy, and maintaining transparency in AI operations will be critical in fostering trust and acceptance among users.

6.1.4 Conclusion

The incorporation of AI into personal assistants and smart homes marks a significant milestone in the evolution of how we interact with our environments and manage our daily lives. As these technologies continue to advance, they promise to deliver even more personalized, efficient, and secure living experiences, albeit with an increasing need to navigate the challenges of privacy and ethics. The future of AI in everyday life is bright, offering glimpses into a world where technology not only serves but anticipates our needs, making our homes smarter and our lives easier.

6.2 AI in Entertainment and Gaming

AI's role in entertainment and gaming has not only transformed how we consume content and engage with digital environments but also revolutionized the creation and personalization of media. This segment explores the profound impact of AI technologies in redefining entertainment experiences and the gaming industry, highlighting innovative applications and the future potential of AI-driven entertainment.

6.2.1 Personalized Content Discovery

A. Streaming Services

AI algorithms employed by platforms like Netflix, Spotify, and YouTube analyze vast amounts of data on user preferences and viewing habits to recommend movies, shows, and music, making content discovery personalized and intuitive.

B. Dynamic Content Adaptation

Beyond recommendations, AI technologies are exploring ways to adapt and modify content in real-time based on user reactions and preferences, aiming to create more engaging and customized viewing experiences.

6.2.2   Enhanced Viewer Engagement

A. Interactive Media

AI is at the forefront of developing interactive and immersive media experiences, such as interactive TV shows where viewers make choices that influence the storyline, offering a unique blend of entertainment and personal involvement.

B. Virtual Reality (VR) and Augmented Reality (AR)

AI enhances VR and AR experiences, making them more realistic and responsive. In entertainment, this translates to virtual concerts, exhibitions, and events that offer immersive experiences surpassing traditional boundaries.

6.2.3   Revolutionizing Gaming

A. Dynamic Game Environments

AI generates complex, evolving game environments that react to player actions, creating a unique experience for every playthrough. This includes non-player characters (NPCs) with AI-driven behaviors that provide realistic and challenging interactions.

B. Procedural Content Generation

AI algorithms create endless variations of game levels, landscapes, and puzzles, offering new experiences and challenges for players and reducing the workload on game developers.

C. Player Experience Optimization

AI tools analyze player data to adjust difficulty levels and game mechanics dynamically, ensuring a balanced and engaging experience tailored to the skill level and preferences of each player.

6.2.4 Future Trends in AI-Driven Entertainment

A. Deepfake Technology and Ethical Filmmaking

AI's ability to create hyper-realistic video and audio recordings opens new avenues for content creation, including replacing actors in films or creating new content with past icons. However, this raises significant ethical considerations around consent and misinformation.

B. AI in Content Creation

Advancements in AI will further enable the creation of music, art, and even scriptwriting, potentially transforming creative processes in entertainment. This includes AI-powered tools that assist artists and creators in bringing innovative concepts to life more efficiently.

6.2.5 Conclusion

AI has become an indispensable part of the entertainment and gaming sectors, driving innovation and enhancing user experiences through personalization, interactivity, and creativity. As AI technologies continue to evolve, the potential for even more groundbreaking applications and immersive experiences grows. However, navigating the ethical implications of such technologies will be crucial in ensuring that AI continues to enrich the entertainment and gaming landscapes positively and responsibly. The future of AI in these fields promises an exciting fusion of technology and creativity, offering audiences and players worldwide new ways to experience and engage with content.

6.3 The Future of Mobility: Autonomous Vehicles

The advent of autonomous vehicles (AVs) represents a pivotal shift in the landscape of transportation, offering a glimpse into a future where mobility is not only autonomous but safer, more efficient, and fundamentally transformed. This section delves into the role of Artificial Intelligence (AI) in driving this revolution, highlighting the technological advancements, societal impacts, and potential future developments in the realm of autonomous mobility.

6.3.1 Technological Foundations of Autonomous Vehicles

A. AI and Machine Learning

At the core of autonomous driving technology are sophisticated AI and machine learning algorithms that enable vehicles to perceive their environment, make decisions, and navigate complex traffic scenarios without human intervention. These systems process data from an array of sensors, including LIDAR, radar, cameras, and GPS, to understand the vehicle's surroundings accurately.

B. Deep Neural Networks for Decision Making

Autonomous vehicles rely on deep neural networks to interpret sensor data, recognize objects, predict the actions of other road users, and make real-time navigation decisions. This AI-driven approach allows AVs to adapt to diverse and dynamic driving conditions.

6.3.2 Impact on Society and Urban Environments

A. Enhancing Road Safety

By reducing the potential for human error, which is a leading cause of accidents, autonomous vehicles have the potential to significantly improve road safety. AI systems do not suffer from distractions, fatigue, or impairment, offering a level of consistency and vigilance unattainable by human drivers.

B. Transforming Urban Mobility

AVs promise to reshape urban mobility, potentially reducing the need for personal car ownership in favor of shared, autonomous transportation services. This shift could lead to decreased traffic congestion, lower emissions, and the repurposing of urban space currently devoted to parking.

6.3.3   Challenges and Considerations for the Future

A. Ethical and Regulatory Frameworks

The deployment of autonomous vehicles raises complex ethical and regulatory questions, such as how AVs should make decisions in unavoidable accident scenarios. Establishing comprehensive legal and ethical frameworks is crucial for addressing liability issues and ensuring public trust in AV technology.

B. Technological and Infrastructure Advances

Achieving full autonomy requires further advancements in AI and sensor technologies, as well as significant investments in infrastructure to support vehicle-to-vehicle (V2V) and vehicle-to-infrastructure (V2I) communications. Overcoming these technical challenges is essential for the widespread adoption of AVs.

6.3.4   Looking Ahead: The Road to Autonomous Futures

A.   Integration with Smart City Initiatives

Autonomous vehicles will likely play a key role in smart city ecosystems, where they can be integrated with other modes of transportation and city infrastructure to create a seamless, efficient urban mobility experience.

B. Advancements in AI and Computing Power

Continued innovation in AI, computing hardware, and connectivity will drive the evolution of autonomous vehicles, making them smarter, safer, and more capable of handling the complexities of real-world driving.

6.3.5 Conclusion

The future of mobility, shaped by the advancement of autonomous vehicles, stands at the cusp of a major transformation. As AI continues to evolve, it promises to unlock unprecedented levels of safety, efficiency, and convenience in transportation. However, realizing this potential requires not only technological innovation but also thoughtful consideration of ethical, regulatory, and societal implications. As we navigate the road ahead, the collaborative efforts of technologists, policymakers, and communities will be pivotal in steering the future of autonomous mobility towards a vision that enhances the well-being of society and the environment.

Chapter Review

6.1 Personal Assistants and Smart Homes

1. Evolution of Personal Assistants

- From Simple Tasks to Complex Interactions: AI-powered personal assistants, embedded in smartphones and smart speakers, have evolved from performing simple commands to managing complex tasks. They can schedule appointments, send messages, make calls, and even provide personalized recommendations, all through natural language processing (NLP) technologies.

2. Smart Home Integration

- Automated Home Ecosystems: AI is at the heart of smart home technology, enabling devices to communicate with each other, learn from user behaviors, and make decisions that optimize comfort, security, and energy efficiency. From smart thermostats that adjust temperatures based on your routines to security cameras with facial recognition, AI makes homes safer and more responsive to our needs.

6.2 AI in Entertainment and Gaming

1. Content Personalization

- Curated Experiences: In entertainment platforms like streaming services, AI algorithms analyze viewing habits to recommend movies, shows, and music tailored to individual tastes, transforming how content is discovered and consumed.

2. Interactive and Immersive Gaming

- Enhancing Realism and Engagement: In gaming, AI generates dynamic environments and non-player character (NPC) behaviors that respond to player actions, creating more immersive and realistic experiences. Procedural content generation powered by AI also allows for endless variations in game worlds, enhancing replay value.

6.3 The Future of Mobility: Autonomous Vehicles

1. Self-Driving Technology

- Revolutionizing Transportation: Autonomous vehicles (AVs), powered by AI, are set to redefine the future of transportation. Using a combination of sensors, cameras, and advanced algorithms, AVs navigate roads, recognize obstacles, and make real-time decisions, promising to reduce accidents, ease traffic congestion, and lower emissions.

2. Impact on Society

- Changing Urban Landscapes and Lifestyles: The widespread adoption of autonomous vehicles will not only change how we travel but also has the potential to redesign urban environments by reducing the need for parking spaces and opening up new possibilities for public spaces. It also offers increased mobility for those unable to drive, such as the elderly and disabled.

Chapter 7: AI in Industry

Artificial Intelligence (AI) is not just a harbinger of a future technological utopia; it is a present-day revolutionizer across various sectors. Its ability to analyze vast datasets, recognize patterns, and make predictive decisions has led to transformative changes in industries such as healthcare, finance, and manufacturing. This chapter explores the significant impact of AI in these fields, illustrating its role in advancing operational efficiencies, enhancing decision-making processes, and creating innovative solutions to age-old challenges.

7.1 Transforming Healthcare with AI

The advent of Artificial Intelligence (AI) in healthcare marks a significant leap forward, offering unprecedented opportunities to enhance patient care, streamline diagnostic processes, and foster preventive medicine. Below is a detailed exploration of how AI is revolutionizing healthcare, particularly through diagnostic innovations.

7.1.1 Diagnostic Innovations

Diagnostic innovations spearheaded by AI technologies have been pivotal in transforming healthcare landscapes. These innovations not only augment the efficiency of medical diagnostics but also significantly enhance patient care quality. Two primary areas underscore this transformation:

A.Image Analysis and Diagnosis

AI-driven image recognition technologies have revolutionized medical diagnostics, significantly enhancing the accuracy and speed at which diseases are diagnosed. This section delves into the critical role of AI in interpreting medical imagery:

- *Advancements in Technology*

The integration of AI algorithms with medical imaging tools such as X-rays, MRIs, and CT scans has led to substantial improvements in detecting and diagnosing diseases. AI systems can identify patterns and anomalies within the imagery that may be subtle or invisible to the human eye.

- *Impact on Early Detection*

Early detection of conditions, particularly cancer, has been one of the most significant benefits of AI-driven image analysis. By accurately identifying diseases at their nascent stages, these technologies offer a crucial advantage in treatment, often leading to significantly improved patient outcomes.

- *Enhancing Precision Medicine*

AI's ability to analyze and interpret complex medical images contributes to the development of precision medicine, enabling healthcare providers to tailor treatment plans to the individual characteristics of each patient.

B. *Predictive Analytics for Patient Care*

Predictive analytics, fueled by AI, stands as a cornerstone in the proactive management of patient health. This section explores how AI algorithms are instrumental in forecasting potential health issues and shaping preventive care:

- *Analyzing Patient Data*

AI algorithms excel at dissecting vast amounts of patient data, including medical histories, genetic information, and lifestyle factors, to identify potential health risks. This data-driven approach allows for the anticipation of health issues before they manifest into more severe conditions.

- *Enabling Preventative Care Measures*

With predictive analytics, healthcare professionals can implement preventative measures tailored to individual patient needs. This could range from recommending lifestyle changes to prescribing medications aimed at mitigating the risk of developing certain conditions.

- *Personalized Treatment Plans*

Beyond prevention, AI's predictive capabilities facilitate the creation of personalized treatment plans. By considering a patient's unique health profile, AI helps in devising more effective and targeted treatment strategies, thereby enhancing the overall quality of care.

In conclusion, AI's role in transforming healthcare, especially through diagnostic innovations, is profound and multifaceted. Image analysis and diagnosis have become more accurate and efficient, paving the way for early detection and precision medicine. Simultaneously, predictive analytics are enabling a shift towards proactive and personalized patient care. These advancements signify a promising horizon for healthcare, where technology and medicine converge to improve patient outcomes and quality of life.

7.2 AI in Finance: From Fraud Detection to Robo-Advisors

Artificial Intelligence (AI) is reshaping the financial sector by enhancing security measures, personalizing financial services, and making sophisticated investment management accessible to a broader audience. This exploration highlights the pivotal roles AI plays in fraud detection and the provision of personalized financial services, marking a significant shift in how financial entities operate and serve their clientele.

7.2.1 *Enhancing Security with Fraud Detection*

In an era where digital transactions are ubiquitous, safeguarding against fraudulent activities has become paramount for financial institutions. AI stands at the forefront of this battle, providing sophisticated tools to enhance security protocols and protect consumer interests.

Real-Time Transaction Analysis

- *Detecting Anomalies*

AI systems are equipped to analyze patterns of transactions in real-time, enabling them to identify deviations from the norm that may suggest fraudulent activities. This capability is crucial in a landscape where fraudsters continually evolve their tactics.

- *Minimizing Financial Losses*

By promptly detecting fraudulent transactions, AI significantly mitigates potential financial losses for institutions and their clients, ensuring the integrity of financial systems.

- *Boosting Consumer Trust*

The efficiency of AI in fraud detection plays a vital role in fostering consumer confidence. Knowing that their financial transactions are monitored and protected encourages customers to engage more freely in digital financial activities.

7.2.2. *Personalized Financial Services*

AI's impact extends beyond security, revolutionizing how financial services are tailored to meet individual needs. From investment advice to portfolio management, AI technologies are making personalized financial planning more accessible and effective.

Robo-Advisors for Investment Management

- *Democratizing Wealth Management*

Traditionally, personalized investment advice was a luxury afforded by the wealthy. AI-powered robo-advisors have changed this narrative, offering customized investment guidance to a wider audience at a fraction of the cost of traditional advisors.

- *Analyzing Financial Data and Market Trends*

These robo-advisors leverage algorithms to analyze vast amounts of data, including individual financial situations and broader market trends. This analysis allows them to propose investment strategies tailored to the unique goals and risk tolerance of each user.

- *Making Financial Planning Accessible*

By reducing the barriers to entry for personalized financial advice, AI-driven robo-advisors play a critical role in financial inclusion. They empower individuals to take charge of their financial futures, regardless of their starting wealth or financial knowledge base.

In conclusion, AI's integration into the financial sector represents a paradigm shift in how security is managed and personalized financial services are delivered. The advancements in real-time fraud detection not only protect financial assets but also enhance consumer confidence in digital financial systems. Simultaneously, the advent of AI-powered robo-advisors democratizes wealth management, making it accessible and affordable to the masses. These innovations underscore the transformative potential of AI in finance, paving the way for a more secure, inclusive, and personalized financial landscape.

7.3 The Role of AI in Manufacturing and Supply Chains

The integration of Artificial Intelligence (AI) into manufacturing and supply chains signifies a monumental shift towards increased efficiency, quality, and responsiveness in industrial operations. AI technologies are pivotal in optimizing production processes and supply chain management, heralding a new era of innovation and competitiveness in the sector. Below, we explore the transformative impact of AI on these areas.

7.3.1. Optimizing Production Processes

AI's role in enhancing production processes is multifaceted, focusing on improving operational efficiency, product quality, and equipment longevity. These advancements are pivotal for manufacturers aiming to stay competitive in a fast-paced market.

A. Predictive Maintenance

- *Minimizing Downtime*

By employing AI algorithms to predict equipment failures before they occur, manufacturers can schedule maintenance proactively, significantly reducing unplanned downtime.

- *Increasing Factory Efficiency*

Predictive maintenance ensures that machinery operates at optimal conditions, which in turn, enhances overall factory efficiency and productivity.

- *Cost Savings*

This approach not only saves on emergency repair costs but also extends the lifespan of the machinery, resulting in significant long-term savings.

B. Enhanced Quality Control

- *Real-Time Quality Assurance*

Machine learning models are adept at analyzing production data in real time to detect deviations or defects. This immediate feedback loop ensures that quality issues are addressed promptly, reducing waste and rework.

- *Meeting High Standards*

The ability of AI to maintain stringent quality control standards across the production line ensures that the final products consistently meet or exceed customer expectations.

- *Waste Reduction*

By identifying and correcting quality issues early in the production process, AI significantly minimizes material waste, contributing to more sustainable manufacturing practices.

7.3.2. Supply Chain Optimization

AI revolutionizes supply chain management by improving demand forecasting and innovating logistics and distribution methods. These enhancements allow companies to be more agile, cost-efficient, and customer-focused.

A. Demand Forecasting

- *Improving Accuracy*

AI significantly enhances the precision of demand forecasting by analyzing complex patterns in historical sales data, market trends, and consumer behavior. This accuracy is vital for optimizing inventory levels and production schedules.

- *Reducing Costs and Waste*

With better demand forecasting, companies can reduce excess inventory and minimize waste, leading to more efficient operations and lower operational costs.

- *Enhancing Customer Satisfaction*

Accurate forecasting also means that companies can improve delivery times and reduce stockouts, thereby boosting customer satisfaction and loyalty.

B. *Autonomous Logistics and Distribution*

- *Transforming Delivery*

AI-driven autonomous vehicles and drones are redefining logistics by offering faster, more reliable, and cost-effective delivery solutions. This technology is particularly beneficial in reaching remote or difficult-to-access areas.

- *Reducing Human Error*

The automation of logistics and distribution processes minimizes the risk of human error, which can lead to delays and additional costs.

- *Sustainability*

Autonomous delivery solutions can also contribute to sustainability efforts by optimizing routes and reducing fuel consumption, thereby lowering the carbon footprint of logistics operations.

In summary, AI's integration into manufacturing and supply chains is propelling the industry towards more efficient, sustainable, and customer-centric operations. From optimizing production processes through predictive maintenance and enhanced quality control to revolutionizing supply chain management with accurate demand forecasting and autonomous logistics, AI is at the heart of industrial innovation. The continued advancement and application of AI technologies in these areas promise to further refine and redefine the standards of manufacturing and logistics efficiency.

Chapter Review

7.1 Transforming Healthcare with AI

1. Diagnostic Innovations

- Image Analysis and Diagnosis: AI-driven image recognition technologies have greatly enhanced the accuracy and speed of diagnosing diseases from medical imagery, such as X-rays, MRIs, and CT scans. These advancements allow for early detection of conditions like cancer, significantly improving patient outcomes.
- Predictive Analytics for Patient Care: By analyzing patient data, AI algorithms can predict potential health issues before they become serious, enabling preventative care measures and personalized treatment plans.

2. Drug Discovery and Development

- Accelerating Pharmaceutical Research: AI models expedite the drug discovery process by predicting how different chemical compounds will react with targets, identifying promising candidates for further exploration and reducing the time and cost associated with bringing new drugs to market.

7.2 AI in Finance: From Fraud Detection to Robo-Advisors

1. Enhancing Security with Fraud Detection

- Real-Time Transaction Analysis: AI systems are capable of analyzing transaction patterns in real-time to detect anomalies that may indicate fraudulent activity, significantly reducing financial losses and increasing consumer trust.

2. Personalized Financial Services

- Robo-Advisors for Investment Management: AI-powered robo-advisors offer personalized investment advice by analyzing individual financial data and market trends, making wealth management services more accessible and affordable to the general public.

7.3 The Role of AI in Manufacturing and Supply Chains

1. Optimizing Production Processes

- Predictive Maintenance: AI algorithms predict when machines and equipment are likely to fail or require maintenance, minimizing downtime and increasing factory efficiency.
- Enhanced Quality Control: Machine learning models analyze production data in real-time to identify quality issues, ensuring that products meet high standards and reducing waste.

2. Supply Chain Optimization

- Demand Forecasting: AI enhances the accuracy of demand forecasting, allowing companies to optimize inventory levels, reduce costs, and improve delivery times.
- Autonomous Logistics and Distribution: AI-driven autonomous vehicles and drones are transforming logistics and distribution, offering faster and more cost-effective delivery solutions.

The application of AI across healthcare, finance, and manufacturing sectors underscores its potential to drive significant improvements in efficiency, accuracy, and innovation. By harnessing the power of AI, industries are not only solving complex challenges but also reimagining the possibilities for future advancements. As AI continues to evolve, its integration into various sectors will undoubtedly yield new opportunities, necessitating ongoing exploration, investment, and adaptation to unlock its full potential. The future of AI in industry promises a landscape where data-driven decision-making and intelligent automation become the cornerstone of operational excellence and competitive advantage.

Chapter 8: Ethical and Societal Impacts of AI

The integration of Artificial Intelligence (AI) across various sectors has ushered in a new era of innovation and efficiency. However, this rapid advancement brings with it a myriad of ethical and societal challenges that need to be carefully navigated. This chapter delves into the ethical landscape of AI, its implications on the future of work, and the crucial aspects of ensuring privacy and security in an AI-driven world.

As AI continues to shape the future of society, navigating its ethical and societal impacts becomes increasingly important. By addressing issues of fairness, accountability, and transparency, adapting to changes in the labor market, and ensuring privacy and security, we can harness the power of AI to benefit humanity while safeguarding against its potential harms. This balanced approach is crucial for fostering an AI-driven future that is ethical, equitable, and inclusive.

8.1 Navigating the Ethical Landscape of AI

The evolution of Artificial Intelligence (AI) has brought about transformative changes across various sectors, enabling advancements previously unimaginable. However, this progress is not without its ethical dilemmas. The ethical landscape of AI is intricate, necessitating a nuanced approach to ensure that the deployment of AI technologies contributes positively to society while mitigating potential drawbacks. Here, we delve into three core ethical considerations central to the responsible development and application of AI: fairness and bias, accountability and transparency, and ethical decision-making.

8.1.1 _Fairness and Bias_

A. *The Challenge of Bias in AI*

Bias in AI systems poses a profound ethical concern, with the potential to reinforce or amplify societal inequalities. These biases often stem from the data sets on which AI algorithms are trained, which may contain historical biases or lack representation from diverse groups.

B. *Strategies for Mitigating Bias*

Combatting bias requires a multi-faceted approach, including diversifying data sets, implementing bias detection methodologies, and fostering interdisciplinary teams that can bring varied perspectives to AI development. Ensuring AI systems are equitable and inclusive involves continuous monitoring and updating of AI algorithms to reflect a broad spectrum of human diversity.

C. *The Importance of Equitable AI*

Developing AI technologies that are fair and unbiased is not just an ethical imperative but also enhances the utility and acceptance of AI across diverse societal segments, promoting inclusivity and fairness.

8.1.2 _Accountability and Transparency_

A. *The Need for Accountability*

Establishing accountability in AI systems is crucial to ensure that individuals or entities responsible for the creation and operation of AI are identifiable and can be held responsible for any issues or damages that arise. This accountability framework is essential for building trust in AI technologies.

B. **Enhancing Transparency**

AI systems should be designed with transparency in mind, enabling users to understand how decisions are made. This involves not just technical transparency but also accessibility, ensuring that explanations are provided in a manner understandable to non-experts.

C. Frameworks and Standards

Developing and adhering to clear frameworks and standards for accountability and transparency can help navigate these ethical challenges, making AI systems more reliable and trustworthy.

8.1.3 *Ethical Decision-Making*

A. *The Role of Ethics in AI*

AI systems, especially in critical areas such as healthcare or criminal justice, must be equipped to make decisions that align with ethical norms and human values. This requires embedding ethical principles into the core of AI development processes.

B. *Developing Ethical AI Frameworks*

Incorporating ethical decision-making into AI involves interdisciplinary collaboration, drawing on insights from ethics, philosophy, sociology, and law. This collaborative approach ensures that AI systems are designed with a comprehensive understanding of ethical implications.

C. Continuous Ethical Evaluation

Ethical AI is not a one-time achievement but a continuous process. As AI technologies evolve and societal norms shift, ongoing evaluation and adjustment of ethical frameworks are necessary to ensure that AI systems remain aligned with societal values.

Navigating the ethical landscape of AI is essential for leveraging the potential of AI technologies to benefit society while addressing the ethical challenges they pose. By focusing on fairness and bias, accountability and transparency, and ethical decision-making, we can guide the development of AI in a direction that upholds human dignity, promotes justice, and respects individual rights. This balanced approach to AI ethics ensures that technological advancements contribute to a more equitable, transparent, and ethical future.

8.2 AI and the Future of Work

The advent of Artificial Intelligence (AI) has initiated a paradigm shift in the labor market and the very nature of work, heralding both significant challenges and opportunities. This transformative period demands a nuanced understanding of how AI impacts employment, necessitates skill evolution, and balances worker empowerment with privacy concerns. Below, we explore the key facets of AI's influence on the future of work, shedding light on job displacement and creation, the evolving demand for skills, and the dual-edged sword of worker empowerment versus surveillance.

8.2.1   Job Displacement and Creation

A. The Dynamics of Job Displacement

AI and automation present a nuanced landscape of job displacement. Roles characterized by routine and repetitive tasks are particularly vulnerable to automation. This shift prompts a reevaluation of certain job functions and the need for workers to adapt to the changing employment landscape.

B. Opportunities for Job Creation

Concurrently, AI fosters the creation of new jobs and industries, particularly in fields such as AI development, data analysis, and cybersecurity. This evolution not only compensates for displaced jobs but also introduces opportunities for economic growth and innovation.

C. The Need for Adaptive Skills

The transition underscores the importance of adaptability in the workforce. Individuals must cultivate a mindset geared towards continuous learning and skill development to navigate the evolving job market successfully.

8.2.2   *Skill Shifts and Education*

A. Evolving Skill Demands

The AI-driven economy prioritizes a blend of technical skills, such as programming and machine learning, and soft skills, like critical thinking and interpersonal communication. This dual demand reflects the comprehensive skill set required in an AI-integrated work environment.

B. Rethinking Education and Training

Addressing the skill shifts necessitates a profound transformation of educational systems. Tailoring curricula to include AI literacy and fostering environments that promote lifelong learning are critical steps towards preparing individuals for the future job market.

C. Bridging the Skills Gap

Initiatives aimed at reskilling and upskilling the workforce are vital in bridging the skills gap. Partnerships between industry, educational institutions, and governments can facilitate access to training programs that equip individuals with the necessary skills to thrive in an AI-enhanced work environment.

8.2.3   *Worker Empowerment vs. Surveillance*

A.   Empowering Workers through AI

AI tools can significantly enhance productivity and job satisfaction by automating routine tasks and providing insightful data analyses. This empowerment allows workers to focus on more complex, creative, and fulfilling aspects of their roles.

B. The Surveillance Concern

However, the implementation of AI also raises concerns regarding workplace surveillance and privacy. The very technologies that can optimize work processes can also be used to monitor employee actions closely, potentially infringing on privacy and autonomy.

C. Maintaining a Delicate Balance

Ensuring that AI serves to empower rather than surveil requires thoughtful policy-making and ethical considerations. Organizations must establish clear guidelines and ethical standards that prioritize worker privacy and autonomy while harnessing AI's productivity-enhancing capabilities.

In conclusion, AI's impact on the future of work is profound and multifaceted, encapsulating both the challenges of job displacement and the opportunities for new job creation and skill development. As the labor market continues to evolve in response to AI advancements, the focus must remain on adapting education and training programs, empowering workers, and safeguarding privacy. Navigating these changes with foresight and ethical considerations will be key to unlocking the full potential of AI in enriching the future of work.

8.3 Ensuring Privacy and Security in an AI-driven World

The proliferation of Artificial Intelligence (AI) technologies has ushered in a new era of convenience, efficiency, and innovation. However, this advancement also poses significant challenges to privacy and security. In an AI-driven world, the imperative to protect individual privacy and safeguard data against breaches and misuse has never been more critical. This section delves into the essential aspects of ensuring data privacy, securing against AI threats, and the ethical deployment of surveillance technologies.

8.3.1 Data Privacy

A. Robust Data Protection Measures

The foundation of privacy in the digital age lies in robust data protection measures. This involves encrypting data, ensuring secure data storage and transmission, and deploying advanced cybersecurity defenses to protect against breaches.

B. Empowering Individuals

It is crucial to empower individuals with control over their personal data. This includes clear and transparent data collection practices, providing users with options to opt-out, and facilities to manage how their data is used. Such empowerment fosters trust and encourages the responsible use of AI technologies.

C. Regulatory Compliance

Compliance with international data protection regulations, such as the General Data Protection Regulation (GDPR), sets a standard for data privacy. Companies must adhere to these regulations to ensure that individuals' privacy is respected and protected.

8.3.2 Security Against AI Threats

A. Anticipating AI Exploitation

As AI systems become more sophisticated, they also become potential tools for conducting cyberattacks. This necessitates the development of AI-driven security solutions capable of anticipating and neutralizing threats posed by malicious AI applications.

B. Continuous Security Evolution

Security measures must evolve continuously to keep pace with the advancements in AI technology. This includes the use of AI to monitor for unusual patterns that may indicate a breach and the deployment of machine learning models to predict and prevent future threats.

C. Collaboration and Sharing

Collaborating and sharing information about threats within the industry and with regulatory bodies can enhance the collective security posture against AI threats. Such cooperation can lead to the development of more robust defense mechanisms.

8.3.3 *Ethical Use of Surveillance Technologies*

A. Balancing Surveillance and Privacy

While AI can enhance surveillance capabilities for security purposes, it also raises substantial privacy concerns. The key lies in balancing the benefits of surveillance with the need to protect individual privacy rights.

B. Establishing Ethical Guidelines

The development and enforcement of ethical guidelines for the use of AI in surveillance are essential. These guidelines should ensure that surveillance technologies are used responsibly, with clear oversight and accountability mechanisms in place.

C. Regulatory Oversight

Governmental and international regulatory oversight can ensure that the use of surveillance technologies adheres to ethical standards and respects privacy rights. Regulations should mandate transparency in the use of surveillance AI and provide avenues for redress in cases of misuse.

In conclusion, ensuring privacy and security in an AI-driven world is a multifaceted challenge that requires a concerted effort from technology developers, regulatory bodies, and individuals. By implementing robust data protection measures, developing AI-driven security solutions, and adhering to ethical guidelines for surveillance, we can navigate the complexities of privacy and security in the age of AI. This balanced approach will enable us to reap the benefits of AI technologies while safeguarding our digital ecosystem against potential threats and abuses.

Chapter Review

8.1 Navigating the Ethical Landscape of AI

The ethical considerations surrounding AI are complex and multifaceted, touching on issues of fairness, accountability, and transparency. Understanding and addressing these concerns is vital to harnessing the benefits of AI while minimizing potential harms.

1. Fairness and Bias: Ensuring AI systems are free from biases is a significant challenge. AI algorithms can inadvertently perpetuate or even exacerbate existing societal biases if they're trained on skewed or unrepresentative data. Efforts must be made to develop AI technologies that are equitable and inclusive.

2. Accountability and Transparency: Establishing clear lines of accountability for AI's decisions is crucial. There should be mechanisms to trace AI decisions back to their creators or operators, ensuring that there's accountability for any errors or harm caused. Additionally, AI systems should be transparent, with decisions explainable to the end-users affected by them.

3. Ethical Decision-Making: AI systems, especially those employed in critical sectors like healthcare or criminal justice, must navigate complex ethical dilemmas. Embedding ethical decision-making frameworks into AI, guided by human values and norms, is essential to ensure that AI actions align with societal expectations and ethical standards.

8.2 AI and the Future of Work

The impact of AI on the labor market and the nature of work itself is profound, with both opportunities for growth and challenges to overcome.

1. Job Displacement and Creation: While AI and automation may lead to the displacement of certain jobs, particularly those involving repetitive tasks, they also have the potential to create new jobs and

industries, emphasizing the need for adaptive skills in the workforce.

2. Skill Shifts and Education: The demand for technical skills, such as coding and data analysis, is increasing alongside the need for soft skills, including creativity and emotional intelligence. This shift necessitates a reevaluation of educational systems and lifelong learning opportunities to prepare individuals for the evolving job market.

3. Worker Empowerment vs. Surveillance: AI tools can empower workers by automating mundane tasks and providing data-driven insights. However, there's a thin line between empowerment and surveillance. Ensuring that AI tools enhance worker productivity without infringing on privacy rights is a delicate balance that must be maintained.

8.3 Ensuring Privacy and Security in an AI-driven World

As AI technologies become more embedded in daily life, protecting individual privacy and securing data against breaches and misuse is paramount.

1. Data Privacy: Implementing robust data protection measures and giving individuals control over their data are crucial steps in safeguarding privacy. This includes transparent data collection practices and the ability to opt-out or manage the use of personal data.

2. Security Against AI Threats: AI systems are not only tools for enhancing security but can also be exploited to conduct sophisticated cyberattacks. Developing AI-driven security solutions that can anticipate and neutralize potential AI threats is vital for maintaining digital safety.

3. Ethical Use of Surveillance Technologies: The use of AI in surveillance technologies raises significant privacy concerns. Establishing ethical guidelines and regulations around the use of such technologies, ensuring they're employed responsibly and with respect for individual rights, is necessary to prevent abuses.

In conclusion, as AI continues to shape the future of society, navigating its ethical and societal impacts becomes increasingly important. By addressing issues of fairness, accountability, and transparency, adapting to changes in the labor market, and ensuring privacy and security, we can harness the power of AI to benefit humanity while safeguarding against its potential harms. This balanced approach is crucial for fostering an AI-driven future that is ethical, equitable, and inclusive.

Part IV: Creating and Managing AI

Chapter 9: Developing AI Solutions

The development of Artificial Intelligence (AI) solutions is a complex and multifaceted process that involves a deep understanding of both the theoretical underpinnings of AI and practical skills in implementing AI technologies. This chapter provides a comprehensive overview of the building blocks of AI development, explores the various tools and frameworks available for AI creation, and outlines best practices in AI project management to ensure the successful deployment of AI solutions.

9.1 Building Blocks of AI Development

The development of artificial intelligence (AI) relies on several foundational components that enable the creation of intelligent systems capable of performing tasks that traditionally require human intelligence. Understanding these building blocks is crucial for individuals and organizations venturing into AI development.

9.1.1 Data

Data serves as the bedrock of AI development. The quality, quantity, and diversity of data play a pivotal role in training AI models effectively. This encompasses both structured data, such as databases and spreadsheets, and unstructured data, including text, images, and videos. Access to large, labeled datasets is essential for training accurate and robust AI models.

9.1.2 Algorithms

Algorithms form the backbone of AI systems, providing the set of rules and instructions that govern how AI processes data and makes decisions. Various machine learning algorithms, such as supervised learning, unsupervised learning, and reinforcement learning, are fundamental to AI development. Each algorithm has its strengths and weaknesses, making it crucial for developers to select the most suitable approach for their specific use case.

9.1.3   *Computing Power*

The computational demands of training AI models, particularly deep learning models, are immense. Access to robust computing resources, such as high-performance CPUs and GPUs, is essential for accelerating model training and experimentation. Cloud computing platforms, such as Amazon Web Services (AWS) and Google Cloud Platform (GCP), offer scalable infrastructure that enables developers to leverage powerful hardware without significant upfront investments.

9.1.4   *Expertise*

Building AI solutions requires a multidisciplinary team with diverse expertise. This includes individuals skilled in computer science, data science, machine learning, and domain-specific knowledge relevant to the application area. Ethical considerations surrounding AI development, such as bias mitigation and privacy protection, also necessitate expertise in ethics and regulatory compliance. Collaboration among experts from various disciplines ensures a holistic approach to AI development and enhances the chances of success.

By leveraging these foundational building blocks, developers can embark on AI projects with a solid understanding of the essential components required to create intelligent and impactful AI solutions.

9.2 *Tools and Frameworks for AI Creation*

A diverse array of tools and frameworks are available to facilitate the development of AI solutions, empowering developers to implement sophisticated AI models and algorithms with greater efficiency and effectiveness.

9.2.1 *Machine Learning Libraries*

These libraries offer a wealth of pre-built functions and modules designed to simplify the process of developing, training, and evaluating machine learning models. Among the most popular are:

A. TensorFlow

Developed by Google, TensorFlow is an open-source library widely used for building and training deep learning models. Its flexible architecture allows developers to deploy models across various platforms, from mobile devices to cloud servers.

B. PyTorch

Developed by Facebook's AI Research lab, PyTorch is renowned for its dynamic computation graph and intuitive interface, making it a favorite among researchers and practitioners alike. It excels in flexibility and ease of use, enabling rapid prototyping and experimentation.

C. Scikit-learn

This versatile library provides a broad range of algorithms for supervised and unsupervised learning, as well as tools for data preprocessing, model selection, and evaluation. Its user-friendly interface and extensive documentation make it an excellent choice for beginners and seasoned practitioners alike.

9.2.2 *Integrated Development Environments (IDEs)*

IDEs play a crucial role in streamlining the development workflow and fostering collaboration among team members. Notable IDEs in the AI space include:

A. Jupyter Notebook

Jupyter Notebook is a popular web-based interactive computing environment that allows users to create and share documents containing live code, equations, visualizations, and narrative text. It supports multiple programming languages, including Python, R, and Julia, making it a versatile tool for data science and machine learning projects.

B. Google Colab

Google Colab, short for Colaboratory, is a cloud-based Jupyter notebook environment that provides free access to GPU and TPU resources. It's particularly well-suited for prototyping and experimenting with deep learning models, thanks to its seamless integration with Google's cloud infrastructure.

9.2.3   Cloud AI Services

Cloud platforms offer a wealth of AI services and tools that empower developers to build and deploy AI solutions with ease. Some of the key offerings include:

A. AWS AI Services

Amazon Web Services (AWS) provides a comprehensive suite of AI services, including Amazon SageMaker for building, training, and deploying machine learning models, Amazon Rekognition for image and video analysis, and Amazon Lex for building conversational interfaces.

B. Google Cloud AI

Google Cloud offers a range of AI and machine learning services, such as Google Cloud AI Platform for managing machine learning workflows, Google Cloud Vision for image analysis, and Google Cloud Natural Language for text analysis and sentiment analysis.

C. Azure AI

Microsoft Azure provides AI services that span various domains, including Azure Machine Learning for building, training, and deploying models, Azure Cognitive Services for adding intelligent capabilities to applications, and Azure Bot Service for building conversational bots.

By leveraging these tools and frameworks, developers can accelerate the development process, enhance productivity, and unlock the full potential of AI technology to address complex challenges and drive innovation.

9.3 Best Practices in AI Project Management

Effective project management is essential for the successful delivery of AI projects, ensuring they meet objectives, stay within scope, and are completed on time and within budget. Here are some best practices to consider:

9.3.1 Clearly Define Objectives and Scope:

- Begin by clearly defining the problem statement, objectives, and scope of the AI project. This ensures alignment with business goals and helps prioritize tasks and resources accordingly.

9.3.2 Embrace Agile Methodologies:

- Agile methodologies, such as Scrum or Kanban, are well-suited for AI projects due to their iterative approach. Agile allows teams to adapt to changing requirements, incorporate feedback, and deliver incremental value throughout the project lifecycle.

9.3.3 Focus on Data Quality:

- Data quality is paramount in AI development. Invest in data collection, cleaning, and preprocessing to ensure high-quality inputs for training AI models. Implement data governance practices to maintain data integrity and compliance.

9.3.4 _Ethical and Responsible AI:_

- Incorporate ethical considerations into AI development from the outset. This includes ensuring transparency, fairness, privacy, and security throughout the AI lifecycle. Develop guidelines and policies for responsible AI deployment and use.

9.3.5 _Continuous Testing and Evaluation:_

- Regularly test AI models against real-world scenarios and evaluate their performance, robustness, and ethical implications. Implement automated testing and monitoring processes to detect and address issues early in the development cycle.

By adhering to these best practices, organizations can effectively manage AI projects, mitigate risks, and maximize the potential for success. This approach fosters collaboration, innovation, and responsible AI deployment, ultimately delivering value to stakeholders and driving business growth.

Chapter Review

9.1 Building Blocks of AI Development

The foundation of AI development rests on several key components that enable the creation of intelligent systems capable of performing tasks that typically require human intelligence. Understanding these building blocks is essential for anyone looking to develop AI solutions.

- Data: Data is the cornerstone of AI development. Quality, quantity, and variety of data are crucial for training AI models effectively. This includes structured data (e.g., databases) and unstructured data (e.g., text, images).
- Algorithms: Algorithms are the set of rules and instructions that AI systems follow to process data and make decisions. Machine learning algorithms, including supervised learning,

unsupervised learning, and reinforcement learning, are fundamental to developing adaptive AI systems.
- Computing Power: The computational requirements for training AI models, especially deep learning models, are significant. Access to powerful computing resources, either on-premises or through cloud services, is essential for efficient AI development.
- Expertise: A multidisciplinary team with expertise in computer science, data science, domain-specific knowledge, and ethical considerations is vital for the successful development of AI solutions.

9.2 Tools and Frameworks for AI Creation

A wide range of tools and frameworks are available to support the development of AI solutions, making it easier for developers to implement complex AI models and algorithms.

- Machine Learning Libraries: Libraries such as TensorFlow, PyTorch, and scikit-learn offer pre-built functions and modules for designing, training, and testing machine learning models.
- Integrated Development Environments (IDEs): IDEs like Jupyter Notebook and Google Colab provide interactive coding environments that are especially useful for data exploration, visualization, and machine learning projects.
- Cloud AI Services: Cloud platforms such as AWS, Google Cloud, and Azure provide AI services that offer scalable computing resources, pre-trained models, and tools for deploying AI solutions at scale.

9.3 Best Practices in AI Project Management

Effective project management is crucial for the timely and successful delivery of AI projects. Adhering to best practices can help teams navigate the complexities of AI development.

- Clearly Define Objectives and Scope: Begin with a clear understanding of the problem you're solving, the objectives of the AI project, and its scope. This ensures that the project remains focused and aligned with business goals.
- Embrace Agile Methodologies: AI projects benefit from an agile approach, which allows for iterative development and flexibility

to adapt to new insights and challenges as the project progresses.
- Focus on Data Quality: Given the importance of data in AI development, invest time and resources in collecting, cleaning, and preprocessing data to ensure high-quality inputs for training AI models.
- Ethical and Responsible AI: Incorporate ethical considerations and responsible AI practices from the outset. This includes transparency, fairness, privacy, and security aspects of AI development and deployment.
- Continuous Testing and Evaluation: Regularly test AI models against real-world scenarios and evaluate their performance, usability, and ethical implications. This helps in refining the models and ensuring they meet the desired objectives.

By understanding the building blocks of AI development, leveraging the appropriate tools and frameworks, and following best practices in project management, organizations can navigate the complexities of creating and managing AI solutions. This comprehensive approach ensures the development of effective, ethical, and impactful AI technologies that can drive innovation and deliver significant value across various domains.

Chapter 10: AI and Global Challenges

In this chapter, we explore how artificial intelligence (AI) is being utilized to tackle some of the most pressing global challenges.

10.1 AI's Role in Addressing Climate Change

Climate change poses a critical threat to our planet's ecosystems and human civilization, but artificial intelligence (AI) holds promise as a powerful tool to address this pressing global challenge.

10.1.1 *Understanding the Significance of Climate Change:*

- Climate change, driven primarily by human activities such as burning fossil fuels and deforestation, results in rising global temperatures, extreme weather events, and disruptions to ecosystems.
- The consequences of climate change are far-reaching, impacting food security, water resources, biodiversity, and human health, with disproportionate effects on vulnerable communities and future generations.

10.1.2 *Harnessing AI Technologies for Climate Solutions:*

- AI, particularly machine learning algorithms and predictive analytics, has emerged as a valuable tool for understanding and mitigating the impacts of climate change.
- These technologies can analyze vast amounts of data, including satellite imagery, weather patterns, and environmental sensors, to model complex climate systems, identify trends, and predict future scenarios.
- AI-driven climate models enable more accurate forecasting of extreme weather events, such as hurricanes, floods, and

droughts, helping communities prepare and respond effectively to these disasters.

10.1.3 *Optimizing Resource Allocation and Sustainability:*

- AI algorithms can optimize resource allocation and energy management to enhance sustainability and reduce greenhouse gas emissions.
- Smart grids, powered by AI, dynamically adjust energy production and distribution based on demand, incorporating renewable energy sources and minimizing waste.
- AI-driven systems optimize agricultural practices, water usage, and waste management, promoting resource efficiency and resilience in the face of climate change impacts.

10.1.4 *Facilitating Climate Adaptation and Resilience:*

- AI technologies support climate adaptation efforts by identifying vulnerabilities, assessing risks, and developing adaptive strategies to protect communities and ecosystems.
- Applications such as precision agriculture, flood mapping, and urban planning utilize AI to enhance resilience and minimize the impacts of climate-related disasters.
- By integrating AI into climate adaptation planning, policymakers, businesses, and communities can make informed decisions to safeguard infrastructure, livelihoods, and natural resources.

In summary, AI offers innovative solutions to address the multifaceted challenges of climate change, providing tools for understanding, predicting, and mitigating its impacts. By leveraging AI technologies effectively, we can work towards a more sustainable and resilient future for our planet.

10.2 Leveraging AI for Global Health

AI is transforming the landscape of global health, offering innovative solutions to improve diagnosis, treatment, and healthcare delivery worldwide.

10.2.1 Advancements in Medical Diagnosis and Treatment:

- AI-powered algorithms analyze medical images, such as X-rays, MRIs, and CT scans, with remarkable accuracy, assisting radiologists and clinicians in detecting abnormalities and diagnosing diseases at an early stage.
- Machine learning models process genomic data to identify genetic markers associated with diseases, enabling personalized treatment plans tailored to individual patients' genetic profiles.
- Natural language processing (NLP) algorithms extract valuable insights from electronic health records (EHRs), facilitating clinical decision-making and predicting patient outcomes based on historical data.

10.2.2 Enhancing Access to Healthcare Services:

- Telemedicine platforms leverage AI technologies to connect patients with healthcare providers remotely, offering virtual consultations, remote monitoring, and prescription management.
- Mobile health (mHealth) applications and wearable devices equipped with AI algorithms monitor vital signs, track health metrics, and provide real-time feedback to users, empowering individuals to take proactive measures to improve their health.
- AI-driven chatbots and virtual assistants assist patients in navigating healthcare services, scheduling appointments, and accessing relevant medical information, particularly in regions with limited healthcare infrastructure.

10.2.3 Disease Surveillance and Prevention:

- AI-based predictive analytics identify disease outbreaks, monitor epidemiological trends, and forecast public health risks,

enabling timely interventions and resource allocation to prevent the spread of infectious diseases.
- Population health management platforms analyze demographic data, socioeconomic factors, and environmental variables to identify high-risk populations and implement targeted interventions for disease prevention and health promotion.
- AI-driven drug discovery and development accelerate the research and development process, leading to the discovery of novel therapeutics and vaccines for infectious diseases and chronic conditions.

10.2.4 *Ethical and Regulatory Considerations:*

- While AI offers tremendous potential to revolutionize global health, ethical considerations, including data privacy, algorithmic bias, and patient consent, must be carefully addressed to ensure equitable access to healthcare and protect individuals' rights and autonomy.
- Regulatory frameworks and standards for AI-driven healthcare technologies play a crucial role in ensuring patient safety, data security, and compliance with ethical principles and medical regulations.

In summary, AI holds immense promise for advancing global health outcomes, providing innovative solutions to enhance diagnosis, treatment, and healthcare delivery while addressing challenges related to access, equity, and ethical considerations. By leveraging AI technologies responsibly and ethically, we can build a healthier and more equitable world for all.

10.3 AI in the Service of Education and Equity

AI has the potential to revolutionize education, making learning more accessible, personalized, and effective for learners worldwide.

10.3.1 *Personalized Learning Experiences:*

- Adaptive learning platforms harness AI algorithms to analyze students' learning patterns, preferences, and performance data, allowing educators to tailor instructional content, pacing, and assessments to meet individual needs and maximize learning outcomes.
- Intelligent tutoring systems provide personalized feedback, guidance, and support to students, fostering self-directed learning and mastery of academic concepts at their own pace and level of proficiency.

10.3.2 *Optimized Curriculum Design:*

- AI-powered analytics tools analyze vast amounts of educational data, including student assessments, curriculum resources, and learning outcomes, to identify trends, patterns, and insights that inform curriculum design, instructional strategies, and educational policies.
- Predictive modeling techniques forecast students' academic progress and identify at-risk learners, enabling early intervention and targeted support to prevent learning gaps and improve student retention and success rates.

10.3.3 *Expanding Access to Quality Education:*

- AI-driven language translation tools facilitate multilingual instruction and content localization, breaking down language barriers and enabling learners from diverse linguistic backgrounds to access educational resources and participate in classroom activities effectively.
- Virtual reality (VR) and augmented reality (AR) technologies create immersive learning environments that simulate real-world scenarios, enhancing student engagement, motivation, and retention of complex concepts, particularly in STEM subjects and vocational training programs.
- Massive open online courses (MOOCs) and online learning platforms leverage AI algorithms to personalize course recommendations, adapt content delivery based on learners'

preferences and progress, and provide interactive learning experiences accessible anytime, anywhere.

10.3.4 *Addressing Equity and Inclusion:*

-   AI-powered educational interventions promote inclusivity and diversity by offering customized support and accommodations for learners with disabilities, learning differences, or special needs, ensuring equal access to educational opportunities and fostering a more inclusive learning environment.
-   Collaborative learning platforms and social learning networks leverage AI-driven recommendation systems to connect students with peers, mentors, and resources, fostering peer-to-peer learning, collaborative problem-solving, and community building.

By harnessing the power of AI in education, we can create more equitable, accessible, and student-centered learning environments that empower learners of all ages, backgrounds, and abilities to thrive and succeed in an increasingly complex and interconnected world.

Chapter Review

10.1 AI's Role in Addressing Climate Change

-   Climate change is one of the most significant threats facing our planet, and AI has the potential to play a transformative role in addressing this crisis.
-   AI technologies, such as machine learning algorithms and predictive analytics, can analyze vast amounts of data to model climate patterns, predict extreme weather events, and optimize resource allocation for sustainability.
-   From optimizing energy usage to facilitating climate adaptation strategies, AI offers innovative solutions to mitigate the impacts of climate change and transition to a more sustainable future.

10.2 Leveraging AI for Global Health

- AI is revolutionizing healthcare by enabling more accurate diagnosis, personalized treatment plans, and proactive disease prevention efforts.
- Machine learning algorithms can analyze medical images, genomic data, and electronic health records to identify patterns and insights that aid in disease detection and treatment.
- AI-powered tools, such as telemedicine platforms and health monitoring devices, enhance access to healthcare services, particularly in underserved communities and remote regions.

10.3 AI in the Service of Education and Equity

- AI technologies are transforming education by personalizing learning experiences, optimizing curriculum design, and expanding access to quality education.
- Adaptive learning platforms use AI algorithms to tailor educational content and activities to individual students' needs, abilities, and learning styles.
- AI-driven educational tools, such as language translation apps and virtual tutors, break down language barriers and provide personalized support to learners of all backgrounds.

By harnessing the potential of AI to address these global challenges, we can create a more sustainable, equitable, and prosperous future for all.

Part V: The Horizon of AI

Chapter 11: The Frontier of AI Research

In this chapter, we delve into the latest advancements and future prospects of artificial intelligence research, exploring the frontiers of innovation and the challenges and opportunities that lie ahead.

11.1 *Cutting-edge Research in AI*

AI research is at the forefront of technological innovation, with scientists and engineers constantly pushing the boundaries of what is possible. Here are some key points about cutting-edge research in AI:

11.1.1 *Continuous Innovation:*

- AI researchers are dedicated to exploring new algorithms, models, and techniques to improve AI capabilities. This involves experimenting with novel approaches and methodologies to solve complex problems more effectively.

11.1.2 *Areas of Focus:*

Cutting-edge research spans various domains within AI, including:

A. *Deep Learning*

Advancements in deep learning have revolutionized AI, enabling systems to learn complex patterns from large amounts of data.

B. *Reinforcement Learning*

This area focuses on teaching AI agents to make sequential decisions by rewarding desirable behaviors.

C. Natural Language Processing (NLP)

NLP research aims to improve machines' ability to understand and generate human language, leading to applications like language translation and chatbots.

D. Computer Vision

Researchers are developing AI systems capable of interpreting and analyzing visual information, enabling tasks such as image recognition and object detection.

E. Robotics

AI-powered robots are becoming increasingly sophisticated, with research focusing on enhancing their perception, mobility, and interaction capabilities.

11.1.3   Remarkable Achievements:

Breakthroughs in AI research have yielded remarkable achievements, demonstrating the power and potential of AI technologies. Examples include:

A. AlphaGo's Victory

In 2016, Google's AlphaGo defeated world champion Go player Lee Sedol, showcasing the capabilities of AI in mastering complex games.

B. Self-Driving Cars

Companies like Tesla and Waymo have made significant progress in developing autonomous vehicles, leveraging AI algorithms for perception, decision-making, and control.

Cutting-edge research in AI continues to drive innovation and shape the future of technology, with ongoing breakthroughs paving the way for exciting applications and advancements in various fields.

11.2 AI's Quest for Understanding Human Intelligence

Understanding human intelligence and replicating it in artificial systems is a fundamental goal of AI research. Here are some key points about AI's quest for understanding human intelligence:

11.2.1 *Ultimate Goal:*

- The ultimate goal of AI research is to develop artificial general intelligence (AGI), which refers to AI systems that possess the ability to understand, learn, and apply knowledge across a wide range of tasks, similar to human intelligence.

11.2.2 *Interdisciplinary Approach:*

- Researchers draw insights from various disciplines, including cognitive science, neuroscience, psychology, linguistics, and philosophy, to unravel the mysteries of human intelligence.
- By studying how the human brain processes information, learns, and interacts with the environment, researchers aim to replicate these cognitive processes in AI systems.

11.2.3 *Challenges and Considerations:*

- Understanding human intelligence poses significant challenges due to the complexity and nonlinearity of the human brain.
- Ethical considerations also play a crucial role, particularly concerning the creation of conscious machines and the potential implications for society.

AI's quest for understanding human intelligence drives research efforts aimed at developing more advanced AI systems capable of reasoning, learning, and adapting in ways that mirror human cognition. While significant progress has been made, many challenges remain on the path towards achieving artificial general intelligence.

11.3. Challenges and Opportunities in AI Advancement

In the pursuit of advancing artificial intelligence (AI), several challenges and opportunities have emerged. Here's a breakdown of these key factors:

11.3.1 Challenges in AI Advancement:

A. Data Privacy

The increasing reliance on data for training AI models raises concerns about data privacy and security. Ensuring the protection of personal information while harnessing the power of data for AI development is a critical challenge.

B. Algorithmic Bias

AI systems can inherit biases present in training data, leading to discriminatory outcomes. Addressing algorithmic bias and ensuring fairness and equity in AI decision-making processes is a pressing challenge.

C. Ethical Concerns

AI technologies raise ethical questions regarding their impact on society, including issues related to job displacement, surveillance, autonomy, and the potential misuse of AI for malicious purposes.

D. Societal Impact

The widespread deployment of AI technologies may have far-reaching societal implications, including economic disruptions, changes in workforce dynamics, and shifts in power dynamics.

11.3.2 _Opportunities in AI Advancement:_

A. Interdisciplinary Collaboration

Collaboration across disciplines, including computer science, neuroscience, psychology, ethics, and sociology, fosters innovation and drives progress in AI research and development.

B. Open Access to Data and Research Findings

Open access to data and research findings promotes transparency, reproducibility, and collaboration in the AI community, accelerating advancements and fostering trust.

C. Development of Ethical AI

Building AI systems that are transparent, interpretable, and aligned with human values presents an opportunity to address ethical concerns and build trust in AI technologies.

D. Human-Centered Design

Emphasizing human-centered design principles ensures that AI technologies serve the needs and preferences of users while minimizing potential harms.

11.3.3 _Importance of Addressing Challenges and Seizing Opportunities:_

- Addressing the challenges and seizing the opportunities in AI advancement is crucial for realizing the full potential of AI in addressing complex problems, driving innovation, and enhancing human well-being.
- By fostering responsible AI development practices, promoting ethical considerations, and engaging in interdisciplinary collaboration, stakeholders can navigate the challenges and leverage the opportunities presented by AI to create a more inclusive, equitable, and sustainable future.

Navigating the complexities of AI advancement requires a concerted effort from researchers, policymakers, industry leaders, and society as a whole. By addressing challenges and capitalizing on opportunities, we can harness the transformative potential of AI to tackle pressing global issues and shape a better future for humanity.

Chapter Review

11.1 Cutting-edge Research in AI

- AI researchers are continuously pushing the boundaries of what is possible, exploring new algorithms, models, and techniques to enhance AI capabilities.
- Areas of cutting-edge research include deep learning, reinforcement learning, natural language processing, computer vision, and robotics, among others.
- Breakthroughs in AI research have led to remarkable achievements, such as AlphaGo's victory over human champions in the game of Go and the development of self-driving cars.

11.2 AI's Quest for Understanding Human Intelligence

- One of the ultimate goals of AI research is to understand and replicate human intelligence, leading to the development of artificial general intelligence (AGI).
- Researchers study cognitive science, neuroscience, psychology, and other disciplines to gain insights into human cognition and consciousness, seeking to emulate these processes in AI systems.
- Challenges in understanding human intelligence include the complexity and nonlinearity of the human brain, as well as ethical considerations surrounding the creation of conscious machines.

11.3 Challenges and Opportunities in AI Advancement

- Despite the remarkable progress in AI research, significant challenges remain, including issues related to data privacy,

algorithmic bias, ethical concerns, and the societal impact of AI technologies.
- Opportunities for AI advancement include interdisciplinary collaboration, open access to data and research findings, and the development of AI systems that are transparent, interpretable, and aligned with human values.
- Addressing these challenges and seizing these opportunities is essential for realizing the full potential of AI in solving complex problems, advancing scientific knowledge, and enhancing human well-being.

In this chapter, we explore the cutting-edge research driving AI forward, the quest to understand human intelligence, and the challenges and opportunities that shape the future of AI development and its impact on society.

Chapter 12: The Future Shaped by AI

In this pivotal chapter, we delve into the profound implications of AI on shaping the future of society, economy, and ethics.

12.1 Visioning the AI-augmented Future

12.1.1 AI Integration:

- AI is poised to become ubiquitous across industries, transforming the way businesses operate and individuals interact with technology.
- Envisioning the AI-augmented future involves imagining seamless integration of AI into various aspects of daily life, from smart homes and automated transportation to personalized shopping experiences and virtual assistants.
- Businesses will leverage AI to optimize processes, enhance decision-making, and drive innovation, leading to increased productivity and competitiveness in the global market.

12.1.2 Automation and Job Evolution:

- AI-driven automation will reshape the nature of work, automating routine tasks and augmenting human capabilities.
- Envisioning the future entails recognizing that while some jobs may be displaced by automation, new roles will emerge, requiring skills in areas such as data analysis, machine learning, and human-machine interaction.
- Continuous upskilling and lifelong learning will be essential to adapt to the changing job landscape and remain competitive in the AI-augmented economy.

12.1.3 Personalized Experiences:

- AI enables hyper-personalization in products and services, catering to individual preferences and behaviors.

- Envisioning the future involves imagining tailored experiences across various domains, including healthcare, education, entertainment, and retail.
- AI-powered recommendation systems, virtual assistants, and personalized learning platforms will revolutionize how individuals access information, interact with technology, and engage with the world around them.

12.2 AI's Potential Societal Transformations

12.2.1 *Impact on Healthcare:*

AI has the potential to revolutionize healthcare delivery by improving diagnostics, treatment planning, and patient outcomes.

Societal transformations include:

- Enhanced disease prevention through predictive analytics and early detection algorithms.
- Personalized medicine tailored to individuals' genetic makeup, lifestyle, and medical history.
- Democratized access to healthcare services through telemedicine, remote monitoring, and AI-powered diagnostic tools.

12.2.2 *Economic Disruption:*

AI-driven automation disrupts traditional economic structures, leading to shifts in employment patterns and wealth distribution.

Societal transformations encompass:

- The rise of the gig economy, where freelance and contract work become prevalent, offering flexibility but also job insecurity.
- The redefinition of work as humans collaborate with AI technologies, requiring new skills and adaptive learning.

- The need for social safety nets, including universal basic income and job retraining programs, to mitigate economic inequalities and support displaced workers.

12.2.3 *Environmental Sustainability:*

AI contributes to environmental sustainability by optimizing resource management, predicting natural disasters, and facilitating climate change mitigation efforts.

Societal transformations involve:

- A shift towards renewable energy sources, such as solar and wind power, supported by AI-driven energy management systems.
- Sustainable urban planning initiatives that leverage AI for traffic optimization, waste management, and pollution control.
- Eco-friendly manufacturing practices enabled by AI-driven process optimization and supply chain management solutions.

12.3 Ethical AI: Guiding Principles for a New Era

12.3.1 *Transparency and Accountability:*

Ethical AI frameworks prioritize transparency to ensure that the decision-making processes of AI systems are understandable and accountable.

Guiding principles include:

- Disclosing the algorithms and data used in AI systems to promote transparency and enable external scrutiny.
- Establishing mechanisms for auditing and assessing the impact of AI technologies on individuals and society.

12.3.2 *Fairness and Equity:*

Ethical AI seeks to mitigate bias and promote fairness by ensuring that AI systems do not discriminate against individuals or groups based on protected characteristics.

Guiding principles include:

- Implementing bias detection and mitigation techniques to address biases in training data and algorithms.
- Designing AI systems with fairness objectives to ensure equal treatment and opportunities for all individuals.

12.3.3 *Human-Centered Design:*

Ethical AI prioritizes the well-being and dignity of individuals by placing human values and interests at the forefront of design and development processes.

Guiding principles involve:

- Respecting user privacy and autonomy by implementing robust data protection measures and providing users with control over their data.
- Fostering informed consent and transparency in AI interactions to empower users and build trust in AI systems.
- Prioritizing the safety and security of AI systems to prevent harm to individuals and society.

Chapter Review

12.1 Visioning the AI-augmented Future

- AI Integration: AI is poised to become ubiquitous across industries, augmenting human capabilities and transforming traditional workflows. Visioning the AI-augmented future involves envisioning a world where AI seamlessly integrates into everyday life, driving innovation and efficiency.

- Automation and Job Evolution: As AI automates routine tasks, it reshapes the nature of work, leading to job evolution rather than widespread job loss. Envisioning the future entails understanding how AI-driven automation will create new job opportunities, foster entrepreneurship, and require continuous upskilling.
- Personalized Experiences: AI enables hyper-personalization in products and services, tailoring experiences to individual preferences and behaviors. Visioning the future involves imagining a world where AI anticipates and fulfills users' needs, revolutionizing sectors such as healthcare, education, and entertainment.

12.2 AI's Potential Societal Transformations

- Impact on Healthcare: AI has the potential to revolutionize healthcare delivery, improving diagnostics, treatment planning, and patient outcomes. Societal transformations include enhanced disease prevention, personalized medicine, and democratized access to healthcare services.
- Economic Disruption: AI-driven automation disrupts traditional economic structures, leading to shifts in employment patterns and wealth distribution. Societal transformations encompass the rise of the gig economy, the redefinition of work, and the need for social safety nets to mitigate economic inequalities.
- Environmental Sustainability: AI contributes to environmental sustainability by optimizing resource management, predicting natural disasters, and facilitating climate change mitigation efforts. Societal transformations involve a shift towards renewable energy, sustainable urban planning, and eco-friendly manufacturing practices.

12.3 Ethical AI: Guiding Principles for a New Era

- Transparency and Accountability: Ethical AI frameworks prioritize transparency in algorithmic decision-making processes and hold developers and organizations accountable for the societal impact of AI technologies.
- Fairness and Equity: Ethical AI promotes fairness and equity by mitigating bias, ensuring equal access to opportunities, and addressing societal disparities. Guiding principles include

designing inclusive AI systems and considering the diverse needs and perspectives of stakeholders.
- Human-Centered Design: Ethical AI prioritizes human well-being and dignity, placing users at the center of design and development processes. Guiding principles involve respecting user privacy, fostering informed consent, and prioritizing the safety and security of AI systems.

In summary, the future shaped by AI holds immense promise and potential, accompanied by profound societal transformations and ethical considerations. By envisioning an AI-augmented future, understanding its societal impacts, and adhering to ethical guiding principles, we can navigate the complexities of AI advancement and build a future that benefits all of humanity.

Frequently Asked Questions

Introduction to AI

What is Artificial Intelligence (AI)?

AI involves creating machines capable of performing tasks that typically require human intelligence. It includes learning, reasoning, problem-solving, perception, and natural language understanding.

How are AI, Machine Learning (ML), and Deep Learning (DL) related?

AI is the broadest concept, aimed at mimicking human intelligence. ML is a subset of AI focused on enabling machines to learn from data, while DL, a subset of ML, uses layered neural networks to analyze complex data patterns.

Applications of AI Across Industries

Healthcare: How is AI transforming healthcare?

AI revolutionizes healthcare by enhancing diagnostic accuracy, personalizing treatments, accelerating drug discovery, and streamlining administrative tasks.

Finance: What impact does AI have on the finance industry?

AI reshapes finance through fraud detection, algorithmic trading, automated customer service, and personalized financial advice, significantly affecting how financial institutions operate.

Education: Can AI improve educational outcomes?

AI personalizes learning experiences, automates grading, and provides analytics to help educators tailor instruction, offering a more adaptive and efficient approach to education.

Agriculture: How does AI benefit agriculture?

AI increases agricultural productivity by optimizing planting, pest control, and harvesting processes through data analysis, predictive modeling, and automation technologies.

Manufacturing: What role does AI play in manufacturing?

In manufacturing, AI improves efficiency and quality through predictive maintenance, real-time monitoring, and automation of production processes, driving innovation and competitiveness.

AI in Business and Economics

Marketing: How does AI influence marketing strategies?

AI personalizes marketing efforts and enhances customer engagement through data analysis, targeted advertising, and automated chatbots, transforming the marketing landscape.

Supply Chain Management: What advantages does AI offer in supply chain management?

AI enhances supply chain efficiency by forecasting demand, optimizing logistics, and managing inventories, reducing costs, and improving delivery times.

Societal Implications of AI

Ethical Concerns: What ethical issues are associated with AI?

AI raises ethical issues related to privacy, bias, transparency, and job displacement, necessitating careful consideration and the establishment of guidelines to ensure responsible use.

Bias Mitigation: How can AI bias be addressed?

Addressing AI bias requires diverse and representative data, ethical development practices, transparency in AI systems, and ongoing evaluation for fairness and accuracy.

The Future of AI & Education

Emerging Trends: What are the latest trends in AI?

Emerging trends in AI include quantum computing, AI in edge computing, advancements in natural language processing, and AI for social good, reflecting the field's dynamic evolution.

Education and Careers: How is AI shaping the future of education and careers?

AI is creating new career opportunities and transforming education through adaptive learning technologies and curricula designed to prepare students for a future integrated with AI technologies.

Future Evolution: How will AI evolve in the coming years?

AI is expected to become more integrated into everyday life, with advancements in AI-human collaboration, ethical AI development, and personalized AI services, shaping a future where AI enhances human capabilities and experiences.

This organized overview offers a comprehensive exploration of AI, addressing its fundamental aspects, diverse applications, business implications, societal impacts, and prospective developments, providing a clear and detailed perspective on the significance of AI in various domains.

Conclusion

As we draw the curtains on this exploration into the vast and intricate realm of Artificial Intelligence (AI), it is imperative to take a moment to reflect on the ground we've covered and the horizons yet to be reached. This book has journeyed through the genesis, the technical backbone, its diverse applications, ethical landscapes, and the promising yet unpredictable future of AI. In doing so, it has aimed to demystify AI, providing a comprehensive understanding that balances both the technical intricacies and the broader societal implications.

Reflecting on AI's Evolution

We began our journey by tracing AI's historical roots, from the early fascination with creating intelligent machines to the groundbreaking innovations that have defined its path. The stories of pioneers and visionaries who laid the foundational stones of this field have not only inspired but also reminded us of the relentless human pursuit of knowledge and progress.

The Technical Backbone and Its Capacities

Diving into the technical essence of AI, we unpacked the mechanisms of machine learning, deep learning, and other pivotal technologies that drive AI's capabilities. This exploration revealed the complexities and the ingenuity behind AI systems that seamlessly integrate into various aspects of our lives and industries, transforming them in ways previously unimaginable.

AI's Multifaceted Applications

The narrative then transitioned into a vivid tapestry of AI applications, showcasing its transformative power across healthcare, finance, education, agriculture, entertainment, and more. Each story, each example, illustrates AI's potential to enhance efficiency, solve age-old challenges, and open new frontiers of innovation.

Navigating Ethical and Societal Terrains

Acknowledging the power of AI also prompted us to confront its ethical and societal implications. This book has not shied away from the tough questions about privacy, bias, accountability, and the future of work. These discussions are crucial in guiding the responsible development and deployment of AI technologies, ensuring they serve the greater good.

Looking Ahead: The Future Shaped by AI

In contemplating AI's future, we've envisioned a world where AI not only augments human capabilities but also drives us towards a more sustainable, equitable, and understanding society. The potential transformations in healthcare, economy, education, and environmental sustainability reflect a future where AI acts as a catalyst for comprehensive societal betterment.

A Journey That Continues

This conclusion is not an end but a pause in the ongoing conversation about AI. As AI continues to evolve, so too will our understanding, our ethical frameworks, and our societal norms. It's a journey that each of us—researchers, practitioners, policymakers, and citizens—partakes in, shaping the trajectory of AI towards a future we aspire to.

Epilogue: The Continuous Learning Path

The Epilogue, Appendices, and Recommended Resources provided in this book are designed to be a compass for those who wish to delve deeper into the world of AI, offering guidance for continued learning and exploration. They serve as a bridge connecting the curious mind to the vast landscapes of knowledge that lie ahead.

As we stand on the brink of new discoveries and challenges, it is our collective wisdom, ethics, and creativity that will steer the course of AI towards a horizon filled with promise and potential. Let us move forward with a sense of responsibility, curiosity, and optimism, ready to play our part in the grand narrative of AI, a narrative that we continue to write together.

Epilogue

Reflecting on the journey through the world of AI, we find ourselves at a pivotal moment in history where the possibilities and potential of artificial intelligence are boundless. Throughout this exploration, we have delved into the depths of AI's capabilities, its impact on society, and the ethical considerations that accompany its advancement.

1. Reflecting on the Journey: As we look back on our exploration of AI, we are reminded of the incredible strides that have been made in this field. From its humble beginnings to its current state, AI has undergone a remarkable evolution, transforming from a theoretical concept to a tangible reality that permeates nearly every aspect of our lives.

2. The Ongoing Evolution of AI: Yet, even as we reflect on the progress we have made, we are acutely aware that the journey is far from over. AI continues to evolve at an unprecedented pace, driven by relentless innovation and a quest for greater understanding. From advancements in machine learning and deep learning to breakthroughs in natural language processing and computer vision, the possibilities for AI are seemingly endless.

3. Significance for the Future: Looking ahead, the significance of AI for the future cannot be overstated. As AI technologies become increasingly integrated into our daily lives, they have the potential to reshape industries, revolutionize healthcare, and address some of the most pressing challenges facing humanity. However, with this potential comes responsibility – a responsibility to ensure that AI is developed and deployed ethically, responsibly, and with the best interests of society in mind.

In closing, the journey through the world of AI is both exhilarating and humbling. It is a journey marked by discovery, innovation, and the endless pursuit of knowledge. As we continue to navigate the ever-changing landscape of AI, let us do so with curiosity, integrity, and a commitment to harnessing its power for the betterment of humanity.

Appendices

I. Glossary of AI Terms A to Z

Here's a glossary of AI terms from A to Z:

A

-   Artificial Intelligence (AI): The simulation of human intelligence processes by machines, particularly computer systems, to perform tasks that typically require human intelligence.
-   Algorithm: A step-by-step procedure or set of rules for solving a problem or performing a task, often implemented as computer programs in the context of AI.
-   Augmented Intelligence: The concept of enhancing human intelligence with artificial intelligence technologies to improve decision-making and problem-solving abilities.

B

-   Big Data: Extremely large datasets that may be analyzed computationally to reveal patterns, trends, and associations, especially relating to human behavior and interactions.

C

-   Computer Vision: The field of AI that enables machines to interpret and understand visual information from the real world, including tasks such as image recognition, object detection, and facial recognition.

D

-   Deep Learning: A type of machine learning that utilizes neural networks with many layers (hence "deep") to learn complex patterns from large amounts of data.

E

- Ethical AI: The practice of developing and deploying AI technologies in a manner that is fair, transparent, accountable, and aligned with human values and ethical principles.

F

- Feature Engineering: The process of selecting, extracting, and transforming relevant features from raw data to improve the performance of machine learning algorithms.

G

- Generative Adversarial Networks (GANs): A class of machine learning systems where two neural networks, the generator and the discriminator, compete with each other to improve the generation of new data samples.

H

- Human-Centered AI: The design and development of AI systems that prioritize human well-being and dignity, placing users at the center of the design process.

I

- Intelligent Agents: Autonomous entities that perceive their environment, make decisions, and take actions to achieve specific goals, often used in AI systems such as virtual assistants and autonomous robots.

J

- Joint Probability Distribution: A probability distribution that represents the probability of multiple random variables occurring simultaneously.

K

- Knowledge Representation: The process of representing knowledge in a structured format that can be interpreted and processed by AI systems, enabling reasoning and decision-making.

L

- Machine Learning: A subset of AI that enables systems to learn and improve from experience without being explicitly programmed, using algorithms to analyze data and make predictions or decisions.

M

- Natural Language Processing (NLP): The ability of machines to understand, interpret, and generate human language, enabling tasks such as language translation, sentiment analysis, and text summarization.

N

- Neural Networks: Computational models inspired by the structure and function of the human brain, consisting of interconnected nodes (neurons) that process and transmit information.

O

- Object Detection: A computer vision task that involves identifying and locating objects within an image or video, often used in applications such as surveillance, autonomous vehicles, and image recognition systems.

P

- Predictive Analytics: The use of statistical algorithms and machine learning techniques to analyze historical data and make predictions about future events or trends.

Q

- Quantum Computing: A type of computing that utilizes quantum-mechanical phenomena, such as superposition and entanglement, to perform operations on data, potentially offering significant speedups for certain types of computations, including AI tasks.

R

- Reinforcement Learning: A type of machine learning where an agent learns to make decisions by interacting with an environment and receiving feedback in the form of rewards or penalties.

S

- Supervised Learning: A type of machine learning where the algorithm learns from labeled data, associating input data with corresponding output labels to make predictions or decisions.

T

- Transfer Learning: A machine learning technique where knowledge gained from solving one problem is applied to a different but related problem, often used to leverage pre-trained models for new tasks with limited data.

U

- Unsupervised Learning: A type of machine learning where the algorithm learns from unlabeled data, discovering patterns and structures within the data without explicit guidance or supervision.

V

- Virtual Reality (VR): An immersive technology that simulates a realistic three-dimensional environment, often used in conjunction with AI for applications such as training simulations and interactive experiences.

W

- Weak AI: AI systems that are designed and trained for specific tasks, such as virtual assistants and recommendation systems, as opposed to strong AI, which exhibits general intelligence comparable to human intelligence.

X

- XGBoost: An open-source machine learning library that provides an efficient implementation of gradient boosting algorithms, widely used for classification and regression tasks.

Y

- Yield Optimization: The process of maximizing the output or performance of a system, often using AI techniques to optimize resources and processes for efficiency and effectiveness.

Z

- Zero-Shot Learning: A machine learning approach where a model can generalize to unseen classes or tasks without explicit training examples.

II.   AI Resource Guide

1. Books: Curated list of books covering various aspects of AI, including introductory texts, advanced topics, and applications in specific domains.

2. Online Courses: Recommendations for online courses and tutorials on AI, machine learning, deep learning, and related subjects, offered by reputable institutions and platforms.

3. Research Papers: Links to influential research papers and academic journals in the field of AI, providing access to cutting-edge research and breakthroughs.

4. Open Source Tools: Collection of open-source tools, libraries, and frameworks for AI development, including TensorFlow, PyTorch, scikit-learn, and more.

5. Communities and Forums: List of online communities, forums, and social media groups where AI enthusiasts and professionals gather to share knowledge, ask questions, and collaborate on projects.

6. Conferences and Events: Calendar of upcoming conferences, workshops, and events in the field of AI, offering opportunities for networking, learning, and professional development.

III. *Interviews with AI Experts*

1. Dr. Sophia Chen: Renowned AI researcher and professor at Stanford University, specializing in natural language processing and machine learning.

- Insights on the latest advancements in NLP and the future of human-computer interaction.

2. Dr. Raj Patel: Chief AI Scientist at a leading tech company, with expertise in computer vision and deep learning.

- Discussion on the applications of computer vision in autonomous vehicles and smart cities.

3. Dr. Mei Ling: Ethical AI advocate and founder of an AI ethics consultancy, focusing on the societal impact of AI technologies.

- Perspectives on the importance of ethical considerations in AI development and deployment, and strategies for promoting responsible AI.

4. Ms. Elena Wong: AI entrepreneur and CEO of a startup specializing in personalized healthcare solutions powered by AI.

-   Insights into the challenges and opportunities of implementing AI in the healthcare industry, and the future of AI-driven healthcare innovations.

5. Mr. Alex Kim: Data scientist and AI enthusiast, known for his contributions to the open-source AI community and online education platforms.

-   Advice for aspiring AI practitioners on developing skills, staying updated with the latest trends, and building a successful career in AI.

These resources provide a comprehensive overview of AI terminology, learning materials, and insights from experts, catering to both beginners and experienced professionals in the field.

Acknowledgments

I would like to express my heartfelt gratitude to the following individuals and organizations whose support, guidance, and contributions have been instrumental in the creation of this book:

The acknowledgments section stands as a profound expression of gratitude, woven with the recognition of the myriad individuals and groups whose contributions have made this exploration into the realm of artificial intelligence (AI) not only possible but impactful. Reflecting the collaborative spirit and the intellectual generosity of the AI community, this section aims to celebrate the collective journey and the individual paths that have converged in the creation of this book.

1. Gratitude to the AI Community

- At the forefront of this acknowledgment is the vibrant and diverse AI community. From the scholars and innovators to the enthusiasts and critics, their collective wisdom, curiosity, and pioneering spirit have been the guiding light of this exploration. The community's dedication to pushing the boundaries of what AI can achieve serves as the backbone of the insights shared within these pages.

2. Contributors to the Book

- Special appreciation is extended to the direct contributors whose expertise, perspectives, and critiques have enriched this manuscript. Their profound knowledge and dedication to advancing the understanding of AI have been instrumental in crafting a narrative that is both comprehensive and accessible.

3. Technical and Editorial Support

- Acknowledgment is given to the unsung heroes in the technical and editorial realms. This includes the data scientists, AI models, developers, editors, and designers whose meticulous efforts behind the scenes have shaped the final product. Their expertise and attention to detail have ensured the accuracy, clarity, and aesthetic appeal of the book.

4. Engagement and Feedback from the AI Sector

- The broader engagement with the AI sector, encompassing academic institutions, industry forums, and online communities, has provided invaluable feedback and insights. This dialogue has infused the book with a dynamic and reflective perspective, ensuring its relevance and responsiveness to the evolving landscape of AI.

5. Personal Acknowledgments

- On a more personal note, heartfelt thanks are extended to mentors, colleagues, family, and friends. Their unwavering support, encouragement, and understanding have been the bedrock of resilience and motivation throughout the journey of bringing this book to fruition.

6. Inspiration and Aspiration

- This acknowledgment also pays tribute to the inspirations that sparked the curiosity and passion for AI, including seminal works, historical milestones, and the everyday applications of AI that marvel and challenge the world. It is a homage to the past and present contributions that fuel the aspiration for a future where AI continues to enhance human potential responsibly and creatively.

7. Hope for the Future

- Concluding the acknowledgments is a forward-looking hope that this book will serve as both a beacon and a bridge—illuminating the path of AI exploration and connecting diverse minds in a shared quest for knowledge and ethical advancement. The gratitude expressed here is not just for past and present contributions but also an invitation for continued collaboration and innovation in the AI community.

8. Readers and Supporters

- Last but not least, I extend my heartfelt thanks to the readers and supporters of this book. Your interest, feedback, and enthusiasm fuel my passion for sharing knowledge and insights in the field of artificial intelligence.

Through these acknowledgments, the aim is to encapsulate the essence of gratitude, collaboration, and shared vision that defines the journey of AI. It is a celebration of both the individual contributions and the collective spirit that drive the field of AI forward, making strides in understanding and application that seemed unimaginable just a few decades ago.

Thank you all for being part of this journey. Your contributions have made a significant difference, and I am deeply grateful for your support.

About the Book

HowExpert Guide to Artificial Intelligence unfolds the complex world of artificial intelligence (AI), guiding readers through its transformative potential and the myriad ways it intersects with our lives. This insightful tome is crafted to demystify AI for a broad audience, from curious novices to seasoned experts, providing a deep dive into the essence, advancements, and ethical landscape of AI.

- Embarks on a journey with a preface that illuminates AI's transformative path, setting the stage for a comprehensive exploration.
- The introduction offers a clear delineation between AI myths and realities, establishing a foundation for the discussions that follow.
- Traces the historical evolution of AI, highlighting key milestones and the visionaries who have propelled the field forward.
- Breaks down the core technologies underpinning AI, such as machine learning and deep learning, explaining their significance and applications.
- Explores the diverse applications of AI, from enhancing everyday life to revolutionizing industries like healthcare, finance, and manufacturing.
- Discusses the profound ethical considerations and societal impacts of AI, including privacy concerns, job displacement, and the future of work.
- Provides insights into the creation and management of AI solutions, detailing the tools, frameworks, and best practices for AI development.
- Looks ahead to the future of AI research, contemplating the challenges and opportunities in striving for advancements and understanding human intelligence.
- Envisions the future shaped by AI, pondering the societal transformations and ethical principles that will guide the development of AI technologies.
- Concludes with reflections on the ongoing evolution of AI and its enduring significance for the future, encouraging readers to contemplate their role in an AI-driven world.

- Appendices enhance the book's utility with a glossary of AI terms, a resource guide for further exploration, and interviews with experts, offering diverse perspectives on AI's present and future.

HowExpert Guide to Artificial Intelligence is crafted as a dynamic resource for anyone seeking to understand or engage with artificial intelligence. With a balanced blend of technical insights, practical applications, and ethical reflections, this book not only educates but also inspires thoughtful consideration of AI's role in our collective future. It's an indispensable guide for those looking to grasp the complexities of AI and its potential to redefine the contours of human experience.

HowExpert publishes how to guides on all topics from A to Z by everyday experts. Visit HowExpert.com to learn more.

About the Publisher

Byungjoon "BJ" Min / 민병준 is a Korean American author, publisher, entrepreneur, and founder of HowExpert. He started off as a once broke convenience store clerk to eventually becoming a fulltime internet marketer and finding his niche in publishing. The mission of HowExpert is to discover, empower, and maximize everyday people's talents to ultimately make a positive impact in the world for all topics from A to Z. Visit BJMin.com and HowExpert.com to learn more. John 14:6

Recommended Resources

- HowExpert.com – How To Guides on All Topics from A to Z by Everyday Experts.
- HowExpert.com/free – Free HowExpert Email Newsletter.
- HowExpert.com/books – HowExpert Books
- HowExpert.com/courses – HowExpert Courses
- HowExpert.com/clothing – HowExpert Clothing
- HowExpert.com/membership – HowExpert Membership Site
- HowExpert.com/affiliates – HowExpert Affiliate Program
- HowExpert.com/jobs – HowExpert Jobs
- HowExpert.com/writers – Write About Your #1 Passion/Knowledge/Expertise & Become a HowExpert Author.
- HowExpert.com/resources – Additional HowExpert Recommended Resources
- YouTube.com/HowExpert – Subscribe to HowExpert YouTube.
- Instagram.com/HowExpert – Follow HowExpert on Instagram.
- Facebook.com/HowExpert – Follow HowExpert on Facebook.
- TikTok.com/@HowExpert – Follow HowExpert on TikTok.

www.ingramcontent.com/pod-product-compliance
Lightning Source LLC
LaVergne TN
LVHW042336060326
832902LV00006B/203

* 9 7 8 1 9 6 2 3 8 6 2 1 0 *